THE FINANCE OF DIVORCE

Peter Vaines

THE FINANCE OF DIVORCE

PAN BOOKS

First published 1996 by Pan

an imprint of Macmillan General Books
25 Eccleston Place London SW1W 9NF
and Basingstoke

Associated companies throughout the world

ISBN 0 330 34252 5

1 3 5 7 9 8 6 4 2

A CIP catalogue record for this book is available from
the British Library

Typeset by CentraCet Limited, Cambridge
Printed and bound in Great Britain by
Cox & Wyman, Reading, Berkshire

For Christopher, Timothy and Harriet
for whom I hope this book will only
ever be of academic interest.

Contents

Acknowledgements *xi*

1. Introduction *1*

Identifying the problem areas *1*　The professional advisers *3*　Jargon *9*

Judicial separation *17*

2. Taxation of Divorce and Separation *19*

Income tax *19*　Additional personal allowance *22*

The costs of child care *24*　Capital gains tax *30*

Avoiding traps on separation *31*　Inheritance tax *33*

Trusts and why they are important *34*　Types of trust *37*

Taxation of trusts *39*

3. Maintenance *43*

How maintenance is determined *45*　Maintenance pending suit *52*

Secured maintenance *53*　One-third rule *54*　Clean break *56*

Lump sums *57*　Variation of orders *60*

Collection and enforcement *63* Taxation of maintenance *65*

Foreign divorces and foreign maintenance *73*

4. Children *76*

The paramount consideration *76* Child Support Agency *77*

How to avoid excessive assessments *79* Children with means *84*

Tax implications *87*

5. The Family Home *89*

Mortgage interest relief *90* Problems of ownership *91*

Joint ownership *96* Types of order *99*

Tax implications *104*

6. Pension Rights *117*

The problem explained – and some solutions *117*

7. The Family Business *122*

Unincorporated businesses *124* Family companies *133*

8. The Effect of Bankruptcy *141*

The effect of insolvency on maintenance *141*

How to protect the maintenance and the assets *142*

9. Wills *145*

Intestacy *145* Where a will exists *149* Mutual wills *151*

10. Cohabitation *152*

Financial implications *153* Inheritance and wills *155*

Entitlement to maintenance *157*

Pre-nuptial and cohabitation agreements *158*

Cohabitation after divorce *160* Taxation *161*

Addresses *171*

Index *173*

Acknowledgements

I am indebted to my professional colleagues, clients and friends who have provided over many years much of the material for this book. It is the experience derived from working on those problems which has formed the background to most of the text.

My love and gratitude as always to Stella for her unwavering support particularly at those times when prose came before play.

Special thanks must be given to my secretary Susan Slater for her skill and patience in typing and amending endless drafts without a word of complaint; also to Benedict Sefi, barrister at law, for his inspirational qualities and for saving me from the worst of my errors.

P. S. Vaines
February 1995

1. Introduction

Identifying the problem areas

This book is about money. It is about divorce too but it is mainly about money. When a marriage breaks down the problems that arise are serious and wide ranging – and if there is insufficient money to go round they can get significantly worse. The more a couple argue about how much each should have, the less there is to share out. It is the cruellest of ironies that the aggrieved spouse, by claiming more money, will, by the very argument, end up with less – even if they win.

It is often suggested that many couples stay together in a state of increasing unhappiness just because they cannot afford to live apart. The maxim that two can live as cheaply as one may not be entirely true – but two living apart will certainly cost a great deal more than two living together. There is another group of unhappy couples who separate in blissful ignorance (or wishful thinking perhaps) of the financial consequences, possibly similar in number to those who get married for the same reasons. Others stay together because of anxiety about money. Some say that if only they had known what it would be like they would have thought twice about it – but now it is too late. Many are just anxious and uncertain about the financial consequences and that just makes everything worse.

This book is intended to explain how the financial side of divorce works, what happens (which is not always what is supposed to happen) so that these uncertainties may be reduced. This will not necessarily diminish your anxiety but you will be better informed about the financial quagmire into which you may be about to tread.

You may not avoid the arguments or the bitterness or a good dollop of professional costs – they are practically inevitable; however, you might avoid the disappointments which arise from false hopes by pursuing a hopeless argument or from failing to pursue a good one.

Every thinking wife knows the tell-tale signs about something being amiss. For example, her husband never takes a bath. I do not mean that he has given up on personal hygiene but that he does not appear to bath nor does he appear to need to. The answer may be that he is bathing somewhere else. Another old favourite is the secretary who is 'not quite sure' when her boss is coming back from a trip abroad. There are tell-tale financial signs too. You may start receiving brochures and sale preview invitations to expensive shops such as Aspreys, Harrods, Mappin and Webb or worse Versace or Turnbull and Asser. There may be a reasonable explanation: you may, for example, shop there or have an account there; however, if you don't, you might wonder why these stores are wasting their time sending you their expensive promotional literature. If you are not shopping there, someone else living at your address probably is, and this can be a dead give-away.

The purpose of this book is not to become involved in issues about whether a couple should get divorced or indeed whether they should have got married in the first place. It is merely intended to examine the financial implications of doing so, or not doing so, in order that both sides can be better informed about the position. That will be to their advantage. I also draw attention to areas where particular financial or tax advantages can be obtained which would add to the financial resources of both parties. That too will be to their advantage. But I recognize that in many cases the financial considerations will be secondary to the emotional, social and family aspects and in the long term these things are much more important than money. But if you can get the financial side right as well, so much the better.

Inevitably in a book such as this there are many generalizations. I make no apology for that; it is not a technical treatise but a general guide to the important areas. For this reason I have excluded as far as possible references to legislation and to decided cases – although not completely, because some statutory provisions and decided cases are so important that they cannot be avoided. Matrimonial disputes are always critically dependent on their own facts and you cannot assume that any particular argument I have put forward will necessarily apply in your case. There may be good reasons why not. However, I hope that even where one idea may not be appropriate, another one will be and that the explanations will assist those who are involved in such disputes to find solutions more readily.

I have not concentrated on the particular position of the husband or the wife but tried to draw attention to points which may be relevant to either of them. Sometimes the competing arguments are set out without concluding which is necessarily better. There may be no right answer and each side will simply argue as best they can. Putting forward arguments for both sides may help in achieving a proper balance.

Finally I must add a word for those who are sensitive about expressions of gender. To keep things simple I have usually referred to the wife as being the spouse with limited assets or income and who would therefore be the recipient of payments or assets from the husband – and would therefore be the petitioner. There is reasonable statistical justification for dealing with the matter in this way and to express everything in terms of a neutral gender would impair comprehension. If, however, you would prefer to substitute the feminine gender wherever the masculine gender appears, the sense will generally be unaffected.

The professional advisers

The role of the professional advisers should not be misunderstood. It is their duty to act in the best interests of the side they are representing. The professional advisers will try to do a good professional job – after all, that is what they are being paid for and that is how they earn their living. You will ask them to do the best they can for you and they will get on with doing exactly that – and quite right too; but doing the best for you necessarily involves doing the worst for the other side and that may not be in your best interests. So stop for a moment and think what it is you really want them to do – before their clocks start ticking. If you do not care how much they will charge you then you have more money than sense. A partner at £200 per hour and an assistant at £100 per hour and probably a third lawyer or junior, plus the occasional services of an accountant at another £200 per hour, means that the fees clock up serious money very quickly. Do not just ignore it on the basis that the other spouse will pay. They might be thinking just the same. And remember: even if the other spouse does pay for your professional advisers, there will be less money available for you.

So pause. What do you want your professional adviser to do? The first thing you want is advice. Where is all this going to lead, how much is it going to cost and how much am I going to get by way of lump sum or maintenance? What about the house and other assets and what about the children? What are the means of the other spouse – do you know, can you guess or what? Do not proceed unless you have a clear idea about what you want to achieve.

You really ought to let your solicitor loose to take the necessary steps to find out the precise financial details of your spouse – if only so that you can dispel any subsequent fears that something has been concealed. When you know the details you then need sensible advice about what it is reasonable for you to claim. That does not mean what is the maximum you can demand from the other side. That way lie conflict, acrimony and huge expense. What you would like to know is where you are likely to end up so that you can go there first and not last.

You may feel bitter and vindictive towards the other spouse and want to punish them by being as mean as possible with the financial arrangements. Fine – but then think of the most extravagant and expensive thing you have ever done in your life – and then think how many times you could have done that for the amount it is going to cost you to pursue a vindictive course. And just think what everybody who knows you will think while you are doing it; what the children will think (not what they will say) and what it will do to you. Why not keep the money and go on a world cruise – it will be cheaper and do you much more good.

If your legal adviser has experience of matrimonial law and practice, he will be able to tell you the kind of broad range of financial settlement which is likely to emerge at the end of the day – however long and fiercely you argue. If he cannot say, ask him why not. What has been his experience? If his experience is inadequate for him to make such a judgement, find somebody else. Do not think that a really aggressive solicitor who will duff up the other side will necessarily be in your best interests. You may feel better but you might end up with a much poorer settlement and at much greater cost.

I have deliberately avoided any detailed reference to legal aid. This is for a number of reasons. If you qualify for legal aid, any solicitor you may instruct will be able to advise you in intricate detail on the subject. It is in his interest to do so. Secondly, the nature of the matters discussed in this book is such that legal aid is unlikely to apply but even where it does it will be subject to the statutory charge. That means that although the legal aid funds pay the legal fees (or at least undertake to do so in due course) they will recover all or part of the fees from you out of the assets obtained in the proceedings.

However, there is one reason why obtaining legal aid can be particularly advantageous even if you have to pay it all back at the end by reason of the statutory charge. This is because where legal aid is granted the amount of the legal fees charged is closely controlled and the solicitor's bill will be assessed by the judge who will often reduce considerably the amounts charged. Even if you have to pay them out of the proceeds of the divorce settlement you will get all this scrutiny and consequential reduction in the fees for nothing.

You really ought to try mediation or conciliation before getting involved in all this. The general unhappiness which is an inevitable part of a separation or divorce is made considerably worse by the adversarial nature of the proceedings. This has an effect on the relationships between the parties after the divorce and on their relationships with the children. It is surely worth trying something before you put the gloves on. There is Relate, which used to be called Marriage Guidance, and they may help you find a way to resolve your problems and to stay together. They may not, of course, and you may think it is a waste of time; however it is probably worth going because even if there is no chance of reconciliation, the experience of the Relate counsellors can be very valuable indeed. Whatever problems you face, they have seen it all before, and may be able to help you find a solution. This may not save your marriage but it may help you avoid some of the worst problems and that alone would be very worthwhile.

You should not think that Relate are only concerned with couples whose marriages can be saved. If the relationship is at an end they will recognize it and will assist in dealing with the emotional problems which will inevitably arise in the separation and divorce. This is going to be a seriously difficult time and the fewer problems you have to deal with the better.

The mediation process is different; it is to try to get the couple to sort out their difficulties without a fight. This is obviously of particular importance in connection with the children and money. The idea is to help the couple work together to find a solution that they may both happily accept – with some guidance from the mediator. This may sound blindingly obvious but you should not underestimate that skill of an experienced mediator to identify the key requirements of both sides because in the heat of discussion, points are often missed and the opportunity for a solution may be lost. Any agreement found in this way is likely to be much more lasting and satisfactory for both sides than an order made by the court after a full-scale punch-up.

There is a long list of mediation and conciliation services and any one of them will provide you with details of all the others. Your solicitors, the Citizens Advice Bureaux and Relate will all be able to point you in the right direction.

It must be emphasized that mediation and conciliation are no substitute for legal advice because each spouse's lawyers will want to check carefully the effectiveness of any agreement which might have been arrived at with the help of the mediation service. It may have serious disadvantages or may have big tax pitfalls which need to be resolved; however, the lawyers and accountants can then work together (rather than against each other) to solve the problems to meet the substance of the agreement reached by the parties.

What will be the accountant's role in all this? The accountant may be needed to advise on the figures about who can afford to pay what – but this is unlikely. The solicitor will usually be able to do that quite easily himself. Where the accountant will be valuable is in ensuring that all the tax implications are properly understood and to express a view on the value of any company or business in which you or your spouse may have been involved. The valuation of a business or shares in a family company is a matter where expert advice is required. The accountant will be able to give you an authoritative view and it is better to know early on what sort of figures are sensible, rather than make all sorts of wild assumptions which may lead to disappointments. It may also help to destroy the fantasies of the other side. He may also be able to ferret out other financial information so that you may be confident that your spouse is not secretly tucking money away to your detriment.

In one case the court saw the position like this:

> The court is concerned with the reality of the husband's resources using the word in a broad sense to include not only what he is shown to have but also what could reasonably be made available to him if he so wished. Much will depend upon the interpretation of the accounts, balance sheets and so on which will require in many cases the expert guidance of accountants. It will rarely be possible to arrive at arithmetically exact figures. The court must penetrate through the balance sheets and the profit and loss accounts to the underlying realities bearing in mind that prudent financial management and skilled presentation of accounts are unlikely to overstate the husband's real resources.

When it comes to tax, your accountant is your friend. He may also be the friend of the opposing party because with luck he will be able to structure the ultimate financial settlement in a manner which gives tax advantages to both husband and wife. There is also the possibility of tax advantages which have been needlessly forfeited through ignorance or tax penalties which might inadvertently arise to create a serious dent in the available resources. This should not be regarded as fanciful. Before 1988, when maintenance payments were tax deductible, it was obviously absolutely essential that a tax deduction was obtained for any payments. I recall one occasion when a man had agreed to pay 50 per cent of his income to his former wife, but the way the payments were arranged meant they were not tax deductible. At the tax rate of 75 per cent, his net income was obviously not enough – quite apart from the fact that he was hoping to eat as well.

Where trusts are involved it will always be necessary for specialist tax advice to be taken because the potential for a tax catastrophe here is high. Only the best matrimonial lawyers will be sufficiently expert in the tax implications of trusts to be able to advise fully in this area.

It is not unusual for a situation to arise where one side is seeking a certain sum by way of financial settlement and the other is proposing to pay a somewhat smaller figure. Somebody has to give way – but naturally nobody will and the professional costs will soar. However, if by careful consideration of the tax position the wife can receive what she would have had after tax is taken into account, and the husband can pay what he wanted, after tax reliefs are taken into account, everybody is happy – well, in a manner of speaking. This kind of fiscal alchemy is not always easy but obviously this approach is far more profitable than just shouting at each other.

The accountant may have acted for one of the parties before – and possibly both. If he has acted for both parties it would be sensible for one to seek independent advice because the potential for a conflict of interest is overwhelming. It will be the spouse with the longest or closest relationship with the accountant who will usually keep him. This is a pity for the other but that is too bad. Well, it may not be all that bad. The accountant will have a close knowledge of the affairs of the other spouse and of the business and will therefore be able to assist the court with assessments of needs, budgets, values, etc., as well as details of resources. His professional integrity should ensure that he is open and frank about all these things; if there is any doubt, it might not be a bad idea to remind him of his duty to the court – and of the fact that he will be cross-examined under oath. The accountant who knows all about the business and financial affairs of one of the spouses may be forced to make damaging revelations in court.

Your own accountant will be able to assist in framing the enquiries which might be put to the other side and to interpret the cryptic answers which will inevitably be given. It will also be very helpful to have him examine very carefully any figures which are produced. He ought to be able to highlight possible errors, omissions and inconsistencies which might not be obvious to anybody else. At the end of the day, assuming some kind of consent order will be sought, the accountant should be asked to look at it just so that you can be sure that it does not have any untoward tax effects.

Jargon

When you start getting involved in the legal side of a matrimonial breakdown you will encounter all types of jargon. It can be quite helpful sometimes to know what the lawyers are talking about – after all, it is your future they are discussing and your money they are spending when they speak to you. Under the circumstances a bit of comprehension is not a bad idea.

The first thing to appreciate is that your case will no longer be a divorce – it will be 'a cause'. Having got used to being 'a cause' you will soon get used to being 'a petitioner' or 'a respondent'. For some reason lawyers have different names for the parties depending upon what type of proceedings they are involved in. A person accused of a crime is a defendant but if he is convicted and appeals he becomes an appellant. In a civil matter you have a plaintiff (he is the chap who initiated the proceedings) and a defendant, but again if it goes to appeal the person who is appealing becomes the appellant and the other side is the respondent. In matrimonial causes the person who is seeking the court order is called the petitioner; the other side is called the respondent. Where the petitioner claims that a third party is involved, that third party is also a respondent – that is a co-respondent. Once you get the hang of it there is no particular problem, so do not be put off.

It is no better when you get to court. You may think that you want a divorce or some maintenance but what you will get is 'relief'. The main relief you will obtain is the divorce itself. But it will not be called that either. You will be granted a decree *nisi* which means that you will be divorced after the expiry of a specified period, unless (that is the '*nisi*' bit) something happens to prevent it. At the end of the period you will obtain a decree absolute: that means you are divorced.

You may then think that you can have something by way of maintenance – but no. You will receive 'ancillary relief', that is relief ancillary to the main relief being the actual divorce. Ancillary relief can take a number of forms but usually it will involve a financial provision order for periodical payments or property adjustment. That means monthly payments or a lump sum. It goes on and on like this and you might be forgiven for thinking that all this jargon is designed specifically for the purpose of making sure you have no idea what on earth is going on. If you are in Scotland it is much worse because they have a whole new vocabulary and you need a phrase book. For example:

pursuer = plaintiff
reclaiming motion = an appeal
aliment = maintenance
behoof = for one's needs
vitious intromitter = person who interferes with the property of another without legal authority
pupil = person under the age of puberty under the care of a tutor or curator

Consent order

A Consent order is what it sounds like – an order made with the consent of both parties – rather than one decided by the court with which one (or possibly both) parties will be dissatisfied. However, it remains an order of the court and has the same authority as any other. Apart from the obvious advantage that both sides are in agreement regarding the terms, a consent order can be of wider application because it can include matters which could not be the subject of a court order, for example, undertakings by either side or perhaps an acknowledgement that no claims will be made under the Inheritance (Provision for Family and Dependants) Act 1975. The court will not make the order just because it is agreed. The judge will examine the terms and want to be satisfied that it is fair to both parties.

A consent order does not absolve the parties from being fair and honest in their dealings with each other. A consent order agreed with one spouse failing to inform the other that they were engaged to be married to somebody else will be set aside by the courts as well as any order which is based on misrepresentation or concealment of relevant facts.

Clean break

This sounds easy enough. The idea is that the court will make an order, usually by way of a lump sum or property adjustment order with no periodical payments, which concludes the financial arrangements between the parties and which cannot be varied later, even if the circumstances change. However, there are different types of clean break. There can be an immediate clean break. There can also be a deferred clean break in which the prospect of variation is not ruled out until some period has expired. It is also possible to refer to a clean break where there is some continuing financial relationship – where the property, for example, is retained for occupation by one party but with the other party still having rights over it (see Mesher and Martin orders below).

However desirable a clean break may be (and it is generally regarded as a desirable objective – at least that is what the House of Lords tells us) it has no particular application where there are insufficient resources for a lump sum or other type of conclusive order to be made. Furthermore it is not possible to have a clean break from one's children and the Child Support Agency will not take much notice of it anyway.

Joint tenants: tenants in common

Where property is held in joint names it is usually either held as joint tenants or as tenants in common. The distinction is profound. Where property is held as joint tenants, on the death of one joint tenant his share will pass automatically to the surviving joint tenant and not to his personal representatives to deal with in accordance with his will. The joint tenancy therefore sidesteps the will and any other arrangements for the devolution of the property.

A tenancy in common by contrast means that each holds their partial interest in the property as a separate asset as part of their estate which passes under their will or under the rules relating to intestacy. It does not pass automatically to the other tenant in common.

If you have property owned as joint tenants it is possible to change the ownership to tenants in common. This is called 'severance' and it does not need the consent of the other. It can also happen if by your conduct you have made it clear that you do not want the joint tenancy to continue. This is explained in more detail in Chapter 5.

Maintenance pending suit

This is exactly what the name implies; that is, maintenance payments made during the period prior to the divorce proceedings. It is intended to relieve the hardship which could otherwise arise by reason of a delay in bringing matters to court. One spouse could be in serious financial difficulty and can apply to the court for maintenance in the meantime. The court can make an order for maintenance pending suit at any time after the divorce petition has been filed and can be backdated to that time. The order will expire on the decree absolute.

Without prejudice

If you make a statement or offer in the course of the negotiations on a 'without prejudice' basis, it means that it cannot be referred to or held against you in subsequent negotiations or in any court proceedings. It is really legal jargon for 'off the record' but lawyers take it very seriously. In a legal dispute it has a valuable place because it allows the parties to negotiate freely without weakening their position should the matter end up in court.

Calderbank letter

The general rule in court proceedings is that the loser pays the costs of the other side. However, that rule will not always be applied in matrimonial cases. In one case an order against the husband to meet the wife's costs was set aside on appeal because of the effect it would have had on his ability to pay a lump sum.

In any litigation it is necessary to have a procedure whereby one party can protect himself from the risk of escalating costs on both sides without giving in completely. One way of doing this is by means of payment into court which means that you lodge with the court a sum of money which the other side can accept in full settlement of the case if they choose. If they reject it and the result of the case is an award by the court of less than that amount, it follows that the offer should have been accepted and the other side should not have gone on fighting (and incurring more costs) trying for more. The effect of 'failing to beat the payment into court' is that costs incurred after the payment into court will not be awarded. You would therefore expect to pay the costs up to the date of payment and the other side will pay the subsequent costs.

In matrimonial cases the idea of winning and losing is not so clear-cut and there is no opportunity to make a payment into court to protect the position regarding costs. There is an alternative procedure which amounts to nearly the same thing. It is a Calderbank letter or Calderbank offer which is an offer made 'without prejudice save as to costs' which means that it is without prejudice in the normal meaning of the term, with the exception that it can be brought to the attention of the judge when it comes to dealing with costs. The judge will not know about the existence of the letter until he has made his judgement on the main issues but when it comes to the award of costs he will usually be influenced by the fact that such an offer has been made.

However, do not use this as a blunt instrument. The court retains a discretion over the award of costs and if you make a Calderbank offer, followed by a refusal for all further negotiations, the court could refuse to award costs as a result.

Duxbury calculation

The Duxbury calculation is a method of determining the appropriate figure to be awarded as a lump sum in a clean break situation. It was devised by accountants in the case of Duxbury v. Duxbury to calculate the lump sum which is needed on assumptions as to life expectancy, inflation, expected investment yields and taxation and which would produce enough money to meet the recipient's needs for life on an annuity basis.

There are various limitations to a Duxbury calculation and it should not be assumed that the court would follow it automatically; it will merely be a figure and a formula which the court will consider and it may need to be modified to take into account additional needs such as a suitable home or other reasonably foreseeable consequences.

In addition it should be recognized that all the elements in a Duxbury calculation will be capable of a great deal of argument because they involve judgements about future events – how much the lump sum will increase by normal investment growth and what the rates of inflation and tax will be in the years to come.

Mesher order

This type of order is examined in more detail in Chapter 5, concerning the matrimonial home. It derives from a case called Mesher v. Mesher in 1973 where an attempt was made to solve the problem of providing a home for the children without depriving the husband of the whole of the value of the house. In broad terms what a Mesher order does is to provide that the house is retained during the minority of the children and then sold, the proceeds being divided between the spouses according to their interests in the property. There are a number of variations of a Mesher order and each is designed to achieve the same objective in slightly different circumstances.

Martin order

This is one of the more important variants of a Mesher order dealing with the situation of the wife who would become homeless when the children reach the age of eighteen, when the house needs to be sold. A Martin order would place the house in trust for the wife during her lifetime, or until she remarries or ceases to live there, at which time it would be sold and the proceeds divided between the parties.

Attachment of earnings order

This is a method of ensuring the payment of a debt and is therefore relevant to the obligation to pay maintenance. What happens is that the maintenance payments are deducted by the employer and paid to the court rather in the way that tax under PAYE is deducted and paid over to the Inland Revenue. The court then pays the money on to the wife. This is obviously a very helpful way of ensuring payment – but only if the husband is in employment. If he is unemployed or is self-employed, this cannot be ordered and other means of enforcing or securing the maintenance must be adopted. Until recently attachment of earnings orders needed the debtor's consent but the Maintenance Enforcement Act 1991 gave the courts power to make such an order without the consent of the debtor. This applies equally to the payments to the spouse and the children and continues to operate in conjunction with the Child Support Act 1991.

Anton Piller order/Mareva injunction

These two court orders have been described as the law's two nuclear weapons and it is most unlikely that you will be involved with either of them unless the other spouse is behaving extremely badly – possibly attempting to deprive you or your solicitors of access to funds (or information about means, which could amount to the same thing).

A Mareva injunction is an order granted by the court on the application of one party only which restrains a person from removing assets from the jurisdiction or otherwise disposing of them. The idea is to prevent the other side frustrating the satisfaction of any monetary award that the court may grant by removing or disposing of the assets. Typically, a Mareva injunction will lead to the freezing of bank accounts. It does not deprive anybody of any assets; it merely ensures that they are still available to meet any award that the court sees fit to order.

An Anton Piller order is similarly an order granted by the court on the application of one party only and it allows somebody to enter the premises for the purpose of searching for, inspecting and seizing property which is relevant to the proceedings. It is only given where speed and security are vital to prevent the destruction or disposal of property or documents. Again, it does not provide any particular entitlement to money; it is just a means of ensuring that essential evidence is not destroyed – or to preserve goods that are likely to be the subject matter of an order.

McKenzie Friend

It is most unlikely that you will need a McKenzie Friend but if one is suggested you will have every excuse to look vacant and wait for an explanation. Why a friend of McKenzie should have anything to do with your divorce will be a complete mystery. However, as with many of the earlier examples of orders which take their name from the cases where they originated, so the McKenzie Friend is derived from a case concerning somebody called McKenzie in which something of significance occurred.

A McKenzie Friend is simply a person, not a lawyer (or at least not one acting in the capacity of a lawyer), who stands beside you in the court (without pay – that is why he is a friend) to help you explain to the court what the problem is.

Judicial separation

An alternative to divorce is a decree of judicial separation. Judicial separation is similar in many ways to divorce but there are some very important differences, some of which can be used to great advantage. It has been suggested that one advantage to the husband is that it gives him longer to hide the money. As we shall see, this is not really the case. What a decree of judicial separation means is that the parties are no longer obliged to live together (although they hardly need a court order for that); it is an effective end to the marriage for all practical purposes but it is not so final or irrevocable a step as divorce. It may be a more attractive alternative for those who are concerned about burning their boats; they may hope that maybe, just maybe, things might get better later; it is a sort of halfway house to divorce which can be pursued later if required. An application for judicial separation can be made during the first year of marriage when a divorce is not permitted and may be particularly helpful if there are religious objections (of the parties or their families) to a divorce. The grounds on which judicial separation may be sought are the same as those which apply in divorce to show that the marriage has irretrievably broken down.

The marriage does not come to an end with a decree of judicial separation but the court still has rights to award maintenance pending suit and ancillary relief as appropriate. The fact that the parties are still legally married does not mean that if one were to die without making a will, the surviving spouse would continue to have rights of inheritance over the other's property. In an intestacy, the deceased's property would pass to the family as if the surviving spouse had already died. However, unlike divorce, a judicial separation does not affect the will and the surviving spouse will continue to inherit under the other's will and gain the benefit of the inheritance tax spouse exemption. In the right circumstances it can be a very useful and more financially secure alternative. If neither wants to remarry, and if the children are grown up (or if there are none) there may be no particular need or wish to divorce. They might be on reasonably good terms and providing adequate maintenance is paid (if it is not the court will be able to step in) it might be positively advantageous to stay legally married. There would be none of the ghastly problems associated with loss of pension rights, and in the case of an elderly couple this might be reason enough to avoid a divorce.

2. Taxation of Divorce and Separation

There is a widespread belief that the tax system discourages people from getting married by treating married couples less favourably than couples who merely cohabit. While cohabitants do have some tax advantages which are not given to married couples, the balance of advantage is most certainly on being married. Before looking at the tax implications of separation and divorce it is worthwhile looking at the advantages of being married, as this will assist the understanding of where the problem areas arise.

Income tax

Personal allowance

Every individual, including a husband and wife, is entitled to a personal allowance which for 1995/96 is £3,525. The husband is also entitled to a married couple's allowance which in recent years has been £1,720 although for 1994/95 and 1995/96 the rate of tax at which the relief is given has been reduced to 20 per cent and 15 per cent respectively. The married couple's allowance is available for the tax year in which the marriage takes place but is reduced by one-twelfth for each complete month in the tax year before the wedding day. (Because of this, where in the year of marriage the man is already entitled to the additional personal allowance for children, in respect of a child born to the woman he is about to marry, or from a previous union, it would be better for him to claim the additional personal allowance instead of the married couple's allowance, because it is not subject to any reduction.)

A married woman can claim (without reference to her husband) that she should be entitled to half the married couple's allowance. This gives the wife an unfortunate opportunity to be malicious because she can claim this allowance whether she can use it or not – and it will reduce the amount of relief available to the husband which may have been relievable at 40 per cent. Unless she is feeling spiteful, she would not make this claim where the tax rate on her income is lower than that of her husband. If the husband and wife both agree, the whole of the married couple's allowance can be transferred to the wife and this can be extremely helpful where the wife is paying tax at a higher rate than her husband.

Before 1990 being married could be a positive disadvantage in income tax terms because the income of a married woman was treated as being the income of her husband for tax purposes, and charged at his rate of tax. The husband gained the married person's allowance but that was not much compensation. However, again it is important not to overstate the point. The maximum disadvantage was not all that much – £3,583 calculated as follows for 1989/90:

Wife's income	£23,485	
Personal allowance	£2,785	
Taxable	£20,700 at 25% =	£5,175
Taxable as husband's income	£23,485	
Less married man's allowance addition	£1,590	
	£21,895 × 40% =	£8,758
Extra tax		£3,583

The extra income tax was therefore limited to £3,583 and it only applied where both spouses had incomes over £23,485.

If the wife had her own earnings you could make an election to have her earnings taxed separately (it was unsurprisingly known as a wife's earnings election) so that you gained the benefit of the personal allowance and the basic rate band from her income; however, the husband lost the married man's allowance so the disadvantage was never completely eliminated.

Since 1990 the earned and unearned income of a married woman is taxed independently from her husband's which eliminates the above disadvantages. Furthermore the loss of the married man's allowance has also been corrected. Now there is a married couple's allowance given to the husband but which is capable of being transferred to the wife and this is allowed in full in the year of separation.

This provides scope for tax saving by ensuring that any investment income becomes payable to the spouse with the lowest tax rate. If a husband is paying higher rate tax on his income but his wife has no income of her own, it would be unnecessarily expensive in terms of tax for the husband to receive all the investment income – dividends, building society interest, etc. If, for example, his unearned income amounted to £7,000 he would pay tax on it at 40 per cent, which would be £2,800. If he were to arrange for the income to belong to his wife, the tax would be substantially reduced because the first £3,525 would be covered by her personal allowance and the next £3,200 would be taxed at only 20 per cent (that would be £640) and the balance of £275 would be taxable at 25 per cent (that would amount to £69). So by rearranging the receipt of their income, the tax liability of the husband and wife would be reduced from £2,800 to £709, a saving of over £2,000 – not bad on income of £7,000.

The rules are of course quite strict and you must take care with the arrangements so that advantage is obtained. It is necessary for example to ensure that the wife has the absolute ownership of the assets giving rise to the income – a right just over the income would not be enough.

Again it is important not to overstate the advantage. The income tax advantage runs out where the wife begins to pay tax at the higher rate – that is where her income exceeds £27,225 as under:

Income	£27,225
Personal Allowance	£3,525
	£23,700
Tax on the first £3,200 at 20%	£640
Tax on the next £21,500 at 25%	£5,375
Total tax	**£6,015**
Tax if all charged at 40%	£9,480
Maximum saving	**£3,465**

Additional personal allowance

Years ago there was a tax relief called child allowance which was a special tax deduction for each child. This was abolished in 1979. However there is another relief for children which is often overlooked and this is the additional personal allowance. In technical terms it is called the additional relief in respect of children and is the same amount as the married couple's allowance. It only applies to single parents who have a child or children residing with them for all or part of a year. The relief is a single allowance given each year irrespective of the number of children. It is not enormous; the relief is £1,720 and is given at a rate of 15 per cent only, representing a cash amount of £258. That may not be very much but you might as well claim it if your circumstances fit.

The claimant does not have to be divorced – or even married. What is important is that for the whole of the tax year the individual must not be married and living with their wife or husband. (This may sound odd but if they were married and living together, the married couple's allowance would apply instead.) If the child is the legitimate or legitimated child of the claimant (including step- and adopted children) it must be under sixteen or in full-time education. If the child is not the child of the claimant the relief can still be available if it is under eighteen and is being maintained by the claimant at his own expense.

Where an unmarried couple live together they are entitled to this relief which effectively puts them in the same position as a married couple because the amount of the relief is the same. A married couple would receive the married couple's allowance but no allowance for the children. An unmarried couple receive the additional relief for the child but no married couple's allowance.

Where there is only one child who qualifies for the relief, each of the parents can claim the relief and it will be apportioned between them in proportion to the length of time the child resides with them – or in any other proportion they may agree. This gives the parents the opportunity to obtain the maximum tax benefit from the relief by agreement. If one party has remarried, he or she will not be entitled to the additional relief for the child and this means that it might be able to be claimed wholly by the other party.

One very important consideration is the length of time that a child has to spend with one parent in order that it can be said to reside with them. Short visits may not be enough but where the child has a room and can reasonably regard himself as having two homes. One with each parent, there is no reason why the relief should not apply to both of them. The Inland Revenue accept that where the child spends more than three months with the claimant in the course of a year, the residence test will be satisfied. Where the period is less than one month they will make detailed enquiries but they accept that the test could still be satisfied.

Where there is more than one child and the parents are living apart, each parent can claim the relief in respect of a different child. In that way they can get two reliefs. If the children live with their mother but see their father regularly, perhaps alternate weekends or possibly one day per week and they have a room available to them at their father's house where they keep clothes and other personal belongings, that should be enough to enable the father to claim the relief. He would only claim the relief in respect of one child, leaving the mother to claim the relief for the other.

This relief is surprisingly not very well known and although it is not worth a huge amount, it was worth more in earlier years because prior to 1994/95 relief was available at the highest rate of tax paid by the claimant. There is a six-year time limit so a claim made before 5 April 1996 could generate a tax repayment of £2,719 assuming the payer was a basic rate taxpayer calculated as under. If the payer is a higher rate taxpayer the relief could create a repayment of £4,000:

1995/96	£1,720 at 15%	=	£258
1994/95	£1,720 at 20%	=	£344
1993/94	£1,720 at 25%	=	£430
1992/93	£1,720 at 25%	=	£430
1991/92	£1,720 at 25%	=	£430
1990/91	£1,720 at 25%	=	£430
1989/90	£1,590 at 25%	=	£397
			£2,719

Furthermore, interest would be payable on this repayment which could amount to another £1,000.

The costs of child care

The problems associated with the costs of child care are not confined to those who are divorced or separated but they do assume an extra importance in these circumstances. Crèches or nannies are expensive and anything which can ease the burden is obviously attractive. Unfortunately the taxman is particularly reluctant to allow any tax relief for these costs. This is because the tax rules generally preclude tax relief for such expenditure. If you are employed the rule is that any expenditure for which you would like a tax deduction must be incurred wholly exclusively and necessarily in the performance of the duties of your employment. You might say that if you did not have a nanny or did not pay for a crèche you would not be able to perform the duties of your employment at all, so the expenditure is necessary. Furthermore you could add that the only reason you incurred the expenditure was so that you could work, thereby satisfying the test that the expenditure is wholly and exclusively incurred for that purpose. This sounds fine – except that in tax matters you do have to look at the words very carefully indeed – and in this case the relevant words are wholly exclusively and necessarily incurred 'in the performance of' the duties of the employment. When you incur the expense of engaging the nanny or the crèche, this is not done 'in the performance of' your duties – unless your job is to do a survey on the reaction of people when they are employed as nannies or something similar. The best that can be said is that when you incurred the expenditure you put yourself in a position to enable you to perform your duties properly. Unfortunately that is not good enough. You may say this is a bit tough, unfair and generally not the way things ought to be and you would not be the first to say so.

Nannies

But don't think that the taxman has a particular down on those incurring child care costs. He has no particular discrimination in mind against nannies; the reports of tax cases are full of examples of this test being applied to all types of expenditure where common sense (and some may say common decency) dictates that a tax deduction ought to be made. Two recent cases concerning journalists on a newspaper who were required to read other newspapers as part of their job highlighted the unfairness and unreasonableness of the rules. The cost of the newspapers was only incurred to put the journalists in a position to do their job better. That is not good enough to entitle the taxpayer to relief. How about the employee whose employer insisted that he had a telephone at home so that he could be reached, and could make telephone calls from home, because it was necessary for his job? No tax deduction there either I'm afraid. Or for the training course undertaken by a teacher to improve his knowledge, or the clothing purchased by a surveyor to visit building sites.

As if this reasoning is not bad enough, the Inland Revenue have another argument up their sleeve. They say that when you incurred expenditure on your nanny, this expenditure was not dictated by the requirements of the job – it was dictated by the particular characteristics of the employee. Accordingly, it had nothing to do with the job you were doing, because not every employee who took the job would require this expenditure to be incurred. Therefore it could not be necessary for the performance of the duties of that particular employment.

As an employee you are therefore sunk if you incur the expenditure yourself. No tax deduction is available and the price is therefore particularly high. It may be higher than you think. Let us assume that your nanny is paid £200 per week gross. To be able to pay £200 per week to your nanny you have to earn £339 before tax:

Nanny: gross salary	£200.00
National Insurance payable by you on the nanny's earnings	£20.40
Total cost of nanny	**£220.40**

You therefore have to earn		£339.07
from which you must pay your own NIC	£33.91	
tax at 25%	£84.76	£118.67
Amount required to pay nanny's salary and NIC		**£220.40**

If you pay tax at 40 per cent you need to earn £431 per week to pay the nanny £200 per week gross. If the nanny wants £200 per week net you have to earn an enormous amount to have enough left to pay her. If you are a 40 per cent taxpayer it will take £29,000 of your earnings, £560 per week, to provide your nanny with £200 per week after you have paid your tax, and hers. This is obviously absurd and you need to find another way.

So, what if your employer pays the nanny for you. Without getting too deeply into the fine print of tax law, a distinction has to be made between your employer simply paying your bills and the position where the employer provides you with a service at his own cost – such as a nanny. It can make a huge difference to your tax position. Let us look first at the position where you employ a nanny and instead of you paying her, your employer pays her. What has happened here is that you have a financial obligation which has been discharged by your employer. The payments to the nanny are treated for tax purposes as being payments to you of salary. It is really no different from your employer paying your credit card statement each month – no one would expect that this would save any tax. The general rule is that if you have a financial obligation which is discharged by your employer, the amount is treated as your earnings for all purposes.

However, what if your employer engages the nanny itself and then sends the nanny round to your house to look after your children so that you can come to work? That is entirely different. You have not incurred any financial obligation nor has the employer discharged it for you. Your employer has merely provided you with a service. Assuming that you are paid at the rate of more than £8,500 per annum, this will be regarded as a benefit in kind and you will pay tax on it by reference to the cost to the employer of providing the benefit. That looks like the same thing – you would be taxed on the same amount and you may think that it makes no difference. However, it is not that easy. We have seen that if you pay your nanny personally it costs you £339 of gross earnings to pay her £200 per week. If however your employer provides the nanny and pays her £200 per week (plus National Insurance contributions of £20.40) you will be taxed as a benefit in kind on the cost to the employer of providing the nanny. That is £220.40 on which you would pay tax of 25 per cent, so it will cost you £55. That is an enormous saving and you might wonder whether there is a catch. What it assumes, of course, is that the employer would be prepared to employ the nanny in the first place and pick up an extra cost of £220 per week for your benefit. That seems rather unlikely. If your employer were to do that, he would probably knock £220 off your salary to keep his costs the same. However, it need not be like that. You may simply be offered employment of which part of the terms would be that the employer would provide you with a nanny; the job would not pay anything like as much as it would otherwise have done but providing you did not have the ability to forego the nanny and receive a salary increase instead (i.e. a cash alternative) this would be entirely effective. Indeed, even if there was a cash alternative a saving would still arise because of the way National Insurance contributions are calculated. The NIC rules are not as sophisticated as the income tax rules and they do not charge benefits in kind. So if your employer were to increase his costs by providing you with a nanny in this way, the benefit would be charged to income tax but you would save a significant amount of National Insurance contributions – and so would your employer because he would save his proportion of the NIC.

It could be better than that because of the way benefits are taxed on employees. They are taxed on the basis of the cost to the employer of providing the benefit. If a nanny were to be employed specifically for you, then obviously the whole cost would be attributable to the provision of the benefit for you. However if the nanny were already an employee of your employer and she did other work as well, perhaps on those occasions when you did not need the nanny, you would have a good argument that the cost of providing this benefit for you was only the additional costs of her travelling to your home and the direct expenses incurred in this particular work. On that basis the benefit would be greatly reduced and the tax would be correspondingly lower.

Crèches

Instead of providing you with a nanny, an employer might provide crèche facilities for your child. That could be done in a number of ways and again the way it is done would affect the amount of tax you would pay. If you take your child to a crèche and incur the liability for payment yourself, the reimbursement by your employer would be treated as earnings just in the way described above. If, however, you take the child to a crèche where arrangements have been made by your employer (that is, the liability to pay the crèche was directly incurred by your employer and not by yourself) this would be a benefit in kind for you and you would be taxed on the cost to the employer of providing the benefit. That would probably be the same amount of tax so little would be saved – except that you would save National Insurance contributions on this amount because benefits are not chargeable to NIC; what is more the employer would be free from NIC as well.

In 1990 there was some relaxation in the tax rules relating to child care, the effect of which was to eliminate the taxable benefit on the provision of child care. However, the conditions needing to be satisfied are so difficult that this is most unlikely to be much help. The tax exemption does not apply to child care taking place in any kind of private house or domestic premises and the premises where the child care takes place must be provided by the employer and either wholly or partly funded by him. This means that the employer cannot just make arrangements to send your child to a crèche; it must set up the crèche itself (perhaps with others) and this robs the relief of any real benefit. Large employers can perhaps use this opportunity to provide their employees with a crèche but for smaller employers there is little possibility of this relief being available.

Self-employed

So far we have been looking at the position of employees who require child care. The self-employed have the same problem, although in some ways it is not quite as acute because the flexibility which is naturally associated with self-employment may mean that the child care is easier to arrange. However, the cost will be no less of a burden.

Any self-employed individual seeking a tax deduction for the costs of a nanny or childminding will not be in a materially better technical position than the employee. In fact the technical test is much easier to satisfy but unfortunately in practical terms it is still virtually impossible. It will be remembered that the test for a tax deduction or expenditure incurred by an employee is that the expenditure must be laid out wholly exclusively and necessarily in the performance of the duties. However, for the self-employed the expenditure merely has to be laid out wholly and exclusively for the purposes of business.

It is the 'wholly and exclusively' requirement which will invariably defeat the claim for tax relief. The cost of employing a nanny will not be for the purposes of the business but for the purpose of looking after the children. You might say that unless you could get somebody to look after the children you could not do the work but that indirect reason is not good enough. If you did not eat you would starve to death and would not be able to work either, but that does not make the groceries a tax deductible item.

While that is the technical position, in practice it is much easier for a self-employed person to obtain tax relief for this expenditure. A self-employed person will often work from home (they may work somewhere else as well but they will also be working at home) and their clients and customers will know that they work from home. Accordingly, correspondence, faxes and telephone calls will all be received at home and it will be quite normal for the nanny to undertake some secretarial duties during the day. Indeed some nannies specifically seek that type of work because it provides variety, an opportunity to develop a wider range of skills, and of course more pay.

The Inland Revenue will allow a tax deduction for secretarial help and if that is provided by the nanny, they will normally allow a portion of the nanny's salary. How large a proportion will depend upon the amount of work undertaken and it will be a matter of negotiation. In purely technical terms it is not possible to divide up the cost of employing a nanny and claim just for the amount attributable to the secretarial work. The wholly and exclusively rule means that no apportionment is strictly permitted. However, the Inland Revenue will nearly always allow a proportion to be made on a commercial basis and if they refuse to do so you should complain very loudly – you are entitled to some relief. In 1994 the Inland Revenue announced a specific relaxation in this area – it was not much, but it represented a clear demonstration that they accepted the principle. They impose an arbitrary limit of £1,500 per annum for nanny's secretarial duties but there is no authority for this figure and if appropriate you can always argue for a larger amount. It was a pity that the statement issued by the Inland Revenue did not cover employees who seem to be equally in need of such a tax allowance.

Capital gains tax

Income tax is payable on income and it follows that capital gains tax is a tax on capital gains. Capital gains are profits that you make on selling assets or money you receive for giving up or selling rights. The idea is simple enough. If you buy a painting for £10,000 and sell it for £15,000, making a profit of £5,000, that is the amount on which you pay capital gains tax. Unfortunately it is never quite that simple. For a start everybody, husbands, wives and even infant children, are each entitled to make capital gains of up to £6,000 each year tax free. The figure of £6,000 is known as the annual exemption and it goes up every now and again. The next important point is that values of assets go up with inflation and what this means is that you could end up paying tax even though the value of the asset has gone down in real terms. So you are therefore entitled to increase your cost figure by the retail price index – but only since 1982 when this relief was introduced.

It is a sad fact of life that while gains are always expected, losses frequently occur. It is only fair that if gains are going to be taxed, losses ought to be relieved in some way against gains that you may make. Unfortunately, however, capital losses are only able to be deducted from gains made in the same year or in a subsequent tax year. It is not possible to carry capital losses back against gains made in the previous year. The same way that gains can be created by inflation when there is no real gain at all, when a loss occurs, it is really a much larger loss because of inflation. For example if I bought a painting in January 1983 for £10,000 and sold it in January 1994 for £15,000 I will make a gain of £5,000. However, if during that period inflation was 75 per cent, in real terms I would have needed to sell the painting for £17,500 just to break even. In fact by taking inflation into account, I have really lost £2,500. Before 30 November 1993 I could use that loss to set against other gains but not any more – subject to some special provisions for gains made before 5 April 1995. Indexation relief is no longer able to create a loss.

Avoiding traps on separation

A crucial aspect of capital gains tax with which we will be greatly concerned in the context of divorce and separation is that if you give an asset away it is treated for capital gains tax purposes as having been sold at its market value and tax is levied accordingly. In particular, market value is used whenever the transaction takes place between 'connected persons' which for capital gains tax purposes includes husbands and wives, brothers and sisters and parents and children. This can create some serious difficulties in the most unexpected circumstances as we shall see, so it is well worth grasping the idea so that you can avoid the problem areas.

This is a relief known as hold-over relief which is of enormous value when attempting to save capital gains tax. The reason why hold-over relief was introduced is to deal with the problem on a disposal where there is no consideration such as a gift. As mentioned above, in that case you are treated as if you have sold the asset to the donee at market value and a capital gain will therefore arise. A claim for hold-over relief displaces the deemed market value and treats the donee as having acquired the asset at your original acquisition cost. When the donee sells the asset, he will obviously pay tax on the whole of the gain since your acquisition. Unfortunately however this relief is severely restricted and applies only to genuine gifts where there is no consideration or where the consideration does not exceed the donor's base cost; furthermore it does not apply to all assets but only to business assets and to transfers which are chargeable to inheritance tax.

Married couples do not have to worry about all this because they are subject to a special rule which is that transfers of assets between spouses are treated as taking place at a value which gives rise to neither gain nor loss. This is not an exemption – it is just neutrality. However, it has one very important condition which is often overlooked – it applies only to married couples who were living together at some time during the tax year in which the transfer took place. It does not, therefore, apply to separated couples or those who are living apart pending a divorce; obviously it does not apply to couples who are not married.

This represents a trap for the unwary couple. If a husband and wife separate and, as part of the divorce settlement, an asset such as a holiday home or a portfolio of shares is transferred from one spouse to the other, a capital gains tax liability may well arise. The couple may assume that because they are married, no capital gains would arise in respect of assets transferred to each other because of the no gain/no loss rule; however, they would be wrong. To benefit from this rule it is not enough to be married; you have to be living together as well. Because they are married they are 'connected persons' which means that any transfer of an asset between them is deemed to take place at market value and tax is charged accordingly. So because they are married the tax rules provide that the transfer must be at market value but because they are not living together they do not get the exemption which otherwise would apply to married couples. This is a really harsh rule and it can be very expensive if it is overlooked. The further implications of this problem are discussed in Chapter 5.

Inheritance tax

Inheritance tax is the latest name for death duties. It is charged on the value of your estate at your death. In recent years the rates have been relatively stable; currently the first £154,000 is tax free and everything above that figure is taxable at a flat rate of 40 per cent.

Certain assets such as business and agricultural property are subject to special reliefs but that will not be particularly important in the context of a matrimonial breakdown – at least not unless one party dies. More important is the concept of potentially exempt transfers which means that if you give something away, no inheritance tax arises unless you die within seven years. Providing you survive for seven years the gift (whatever it is) will be entirely exempt. This is subject to one very important exception, which is that you must not retain any benefit from the asset you have given away; if you do it will not be regarded as a valid gift for inheritance tax purposes and it will remain as part of your estate to be charged on your death.

The most significant difference between a married couple and an unmarried couple for inheritance tax purposes is that there is a complete exemption from inheritance tax on transfers between spouses; there is no exemption at all on transfers between unmarried couples. Attempts have been made by cohabitants to claim the exemption on the grounds that the relationship was a marriage in all but name, but none of them work. The answer is that Parliament provided a relief for people who are legally married and unless you satisfy the condition, you do not get the benefit. Tax is a bit like that – but one should not really complain. If you start claiming a tax exemption because you nearly satisfy the conditions, the Inland Revenue may start charging tax on the same basis. For example a husband and wife might be having some difficulties and may be contemplating a divorce. On this basis the Inland Revenue might say that they should be denied the spouse exemption because they are nearly divorced; perhaps they were just thinking about a divorce – or maybe they just had an argument. There is no end to this. The only way tax can operate is strictly by the rules because otherwise nobody knows where they are. Where an unmarried couple are faced with an inheritance tax liability in the event of the death of one of the parties they should think very seriously about life assurance which will at least provide the money to avoid a catastrophe arising on the death of the first party.

Special rules apply for inheritance tax to individuals who are not domiciled in the United Kingdom. If one of the parties has a foreign domicile, professional advice should be sought because there will be opportunities for substantial tax savings which go considerably beyond the scope of this book. However, there are also traps to avoid in transferring assets to a foreign spouse and these must also be carefully considered.

Trusts and why they are important

Trusts are very important indeed in connection with all types of tax and financial planning and they have a particular role to play in connection with the matrimonial breakdown. You will inevitably encounter trusts whether you want to or not and you should not be daunted by them. Trusts are the product of centuries of legal ingenuity and can be drafted to do almost anything you want. Although they are useful vehicles for tax planning they can also provide a valuable role in the preservation of wealth for the family.

Some people are really put off by trusts (perhaps by some earlier experience or by anecdotes from friends) and do not want to have anything to do with them. This is a grave error; it is to place yourself at a considerable disadvantage because many objectives and tax savings will be forfeited and they can run into tens of thousands of pounds (and more) simply because of a failure or unwillingness to understand how trusts work.

In any event in most matrimonial proceedings you will not be able to avoid a trust. Most orders dealing with the matrimonial home, other than one for the sale and distribution of the proceeds between the parties, will create a trust for the benefit of the spouses and possibly the children. If you would like any security for your maintenance, that is likely to be provided by a trust and almost any kind of financial provision for the children (other than that imposed by the Child Support Agency) will require a trust.

Trusts are complicated things but you do not need to worry about all the complications. You watch your television or drive your car without worrying about all the technical background of why it works. If something goes wrong you take it to the menders – or in the case of a trust, to your solicitors. It is however useful to have a broad idea how things are supposed to operate and the following explanations may be helpful.

A trust is an arrangement whereby one person (the settlor) transfers property to another (the trustee) to hold for the benefit of others (the beneficiaries). Trusts are normally created by a formal document signed by the settlor and by the trustees, but this is not always necessary; trusts can be created orally or even by conduct. The rights and obligations of the settlor, the trustees and the beneficiaries are entirely different and should not be confused.

The settlor

The settlor is the person who establishes the trust or anybody who transfers property to the trust. There can be more than one settlor of the same trust. The trust deed will specify the duties and obligations of the trustees, but once the trust has been established the settlor will have no further power over the trustees or the property in the trust. However, the settlor can retain a degree of influence by requiring the trustees to obtain his consent before doing certain things, and he can reserve for himself the power to appoint new trustees. However, the trustees while in office will have the legal ownership of all trust assets, and should be chosen with great care.

The trustees

The trustees must deal with the trust property as directed by the trust deed, and they have numerous obligations imposed on them by law. Neither the settlor nor the beneficiaries can instruct the trustees what to do, although the trustees must at all times act in the best interests of the beneficiaries. If the beneficiaries feel that the trust is being improperly administered, they can seek a court order to put matters right. There is no reason why the settlor cannot be a trustee, although sometimes this will not be desirable for tax and other reasons.

The beneficiaries

The beneficiaries are the persons mentioned in the trust deed as the persons for whose benefit the trustees hold the settled property. They can be specific individuals or a class of persons (e.g. all the present and future children of the settlor) and the trust can make provision for adding or removing beneficiaries from the class. Nobody other than a beneficiary is entitled to benefit from the settled property. The settlor can be a beneficiary, and this will often be necessary to secure tax advantages.

The trust document must be very carefully drawn up, because if there is any uncertainty about the terms of the trust, or if it could last for longer than the permitted period, it may be void and fail totally to achieve any of its intended purposes.

The effect of a trust

The effect of a trust is to separate the legal ownership of assets from those who are entitled to benefit from them. Furthermore, a trust can create a division between the assets themselves and the income which they produce. A beneficiary entitled to the income is usually called the Life Tenant, and a beneficiary who is entitled to the capital is usually called the Remainderman.

These factors can be extremely useful in preserving a family's wealth by ensuring that it remains in responsible hands and does not pass into the control of others who may be too young, too old or otherwise unable to deal with the property satisfactorily, particularly when large sums are involved. Traditionally this was helpful in the case of young daughters to protect their inheritance from the grasp of unworthy suitors, but a trust is equally appropriate to protect wealth from improvident or financially unsophisticated beneficiaries. In modern times this principle has been extended to enable a family business to remain in the control of experienced trustees, so that effective succession by the next generation can be secured at the appropriate time. In the context of a matrimonial breakdown it enables the assets to be used to provide a home or an income for one party without depriving the other of the ownership of the assets. Similarly in connection with taxation, long-term tax advantages can be obtained by the use of a trust without the loss of effective control over the assets.

A trust which is established in contemplation of a marriage is known as an 'antenuptial trust' and this can be important in the context of a divorce. When the court considers the obligation to pay maintenance or a lump sum, one of the opportunities available is to vary an antenuptial trust to provide funds for the purpose.

Reference will also be made later to constructive trusts in connection with property rights. A constructive trust is imposed by the law (whether the parties like it or not) where property is held by one person but justice and fairness dictate that somebody else should have an interest in it.

Types of trust

Fixed interest trust

This is where a beneficiary has a right to all or part of the income of the trust as it arises, without necessarily any entitlement to capital. The beneficiary may only have a right to the income for a limited period, and it is possible for the trustee to provide for the right to be revoked, e.g. if the beneficiary proves unworthy of benefit in the opinion of the settlor or the trustees. The beneficiary with a fixed interest is said to have an interest in possession, which is an important concept for inheritance tax.

The income of a fixed interest trust is charged to tax at the basic rate in the hands of the trustees, and the net amount is paid to the beneficiary. If the beneficiary is liable to tax at the higher rate, he will have further tax to pay on this income.

In some cases there is no income at all and what matters then is the right to the income if any arose. The right to use the assets is regarded as equivalent to entitlement to income so a beneficiary would still have a fixed interest if he was entitled as of right (and not just at the trustees' discretion to use an asset – live in a house, for example, owned by the trustees.

Discretionary trust

This is where the trustees have a discretion to decide which, if any, of the beneficiaries should receive money from the trust in the form of income or capital. This discretion can be extremely wide, although the trustees can be guided in the exercise of their discretion by the wishes of the settlor if necessary.

The income of a discretionary trust is taxed at 35 per cent in the hands of the trustees; if any of the income is paid to a beneficiary, the beneficiary will be treated as having received the income after deduction of tax at 35 per cent. If the beneficiary is liable to tax at the higher rate, he will have to pay further tax directly to the Inland Revenue. If he is not liable to tax at this rate, the beneficiary can claim a tax repayment. In certain circumstances, such as where the settlor retains an interest in the trust, the income will be deemed for United Kingdom tax purposes to be the income of the settlor.

Accumulation and maintenance trust

An accumulation and maintenance trust is a type of discretionary trust, for the benefit of infants and young people under the age of twenty-five. Such a trust attracts particularly favourable treatment for inheritance tax purposes. Usually the trustees will pay income tax at 35 per cent on the income of the trust until the beneficiaries reach the age of eighteen. However, it is important to note that if any income is paid to or for the benefit of a beneficiary who is unmarried and under the age of eighteen from a trust set up by his parents, that income will be treated as the income of the parents for all tax purposes.

Charitable trust

A charitable trust is simply a trust for the exclusive benefit of a charity. Charitable trusts enjoy extensive freedom from taxation, but it is important to appreciate that all the income and capital must be applied for charitable purposes only – and for no other purposes whatsoever. If any possibility exists that the settled property could be used for a non-charitable purpose, it will fail to qualify as a charitable trust.

Taxation of trusts

Income tax

The income tax treatment of the various types of trust has already been mentioned briefly, from which it may be appreciated that the Inland Revenue are able to prevent many of the obvious means of exploitation of trusts for income tax purposes. However, a number of opportunities still remain. If the beneficiaries are not the children of the settlor, it is possible to pay out the income to the beneficiaries each year while they are infants to utilize their personal allowances, and if required their basic rate band. This can be a very substantial advantage, and can provide funds for the payment of school fees at little or no tax cost.

If the beneficiaries are the children of the settlor, this advantage is not available, because the income paid to or for the infant children will be treated as the income of the settlor. However, that does not mean all is lost. In Chapter 4 it is explained how to get round this particular rule.

Capital gains tax

Trustees are liable to capital gains tax on their own gains, and are entitled to their own annual exemption, which is usually one half of the exemption which applies to an individual. This does not apply where the settlor or his spouse has an interest under the settlement, because in that case the gains made by the trustees will be treated as the gains of the settlor and taxed accordingly.

Trustees are charged on capital gains at a rate of 25 per cent, unless any part of their income is chargeable to tax at 35 per cent, in which case this higher rate will apply to capital gains tax as well. Accordingly, an advantage can be obtained by putting assets into trusts which would otherwise be chargeable to capital gains tax at 40 per cent on their disposal, because if the settlor does not have an interest under the settlement, the tax can be limited to 25 per cent.

Any transfers of assets to trustees will be treated as disposals for capital gains tax. Usually the assets will be transferred by way of gift, but will be treated for capital gains tax purposes as if they had been sold by the settlor at market value. Depending upon the value of the assets at the time of the transfer, this may give rise to a capital gain, subject to any reliefs or exemptions which may be available to the settlor.

Some transfers of assets can benefit from hold-over relief, which means that the gain which would normally arise on the transfer is deferred until the assets are sold by the trustees.

When assets are distributed from a trust to the beneficiaries, this is regarded as a disposal at market value by the trustees for capital gains tax, and a charge may therefore arise. Care must be taken in planning such distributions if the settled property has grown in value significantly during the trustees' ownership. A charge can also arise on the occasion when a beneficiary becomes absolutely entitled to part of the settled property. The trustees may be able to claim hold-over relief if the assets are of a suitable nature, but this is a point which needs to be carefully considered, because a tax liability can unexpectedly arise. Cash is not a chargeable asset, and can be distributed to the beneficiaries free of capital gains tax.

Inheritance tax

Trusts can give rise to considerable inheritance tax advantages, mainly by virtue of the separation which takes place in the ownership of the assets and the differing entitlements to income and capital which can be created.

As a general principle, the person entitled to the income from the trust is treated for inheritance tax purposes as being beneficially entitled to the assets themselves. However, in many cases the settlor will not want to continue to receive the income from the assets – indeed, the assets might not give rise to any income. The settlor will often want to remove the assets from his estate, without necessarily giving those assets to anybody else; furthermore, he may want to keep them under his effective control. In these circumstances a trust can be the complete answer. He could, for example, transfer the assets to a discretionary trust for the benefit of his wife and family, thereby giving no entitlement to income to any other person, and the assets would be under the control of the trustees (of which he may be one). This is particularly helpful in the case of private company shares, where the continuity of voting control may be important. For this advantage to be obtained, it is important to avoid the settlor reserving any benefit from the trust.

A transfer to a discretionary trust will not give rise to any liability to inheritance tax for gifts up to £154,000, but beyond that level inheritance tax arises at a rate of 20 per cent, because such transfers are regarded as chargeable transfers. This treatment can be avoided by providing for the beneficiaries to have a fixed interest, giving them an entitlement to income arising from the trust property, but with the settlor retaining the right to revoke their interest and to direct the property elsewhere. This would provide the settlor with the same degree of effective control over the assets as would exist under a discretionary trust, but without any inheritance tax charge arising if the assets involved exceeded £154,000.

A discretionary trust is subject to a charge to inheritance tax every ten years, currently at 6 per cent of the value of the fund, but with careful planning even this modest charge can be eliminated.

The almost infinite variations of the terms of a trust usually mean that all the wishes of the settlor can be accomplished within the framework of a trust, while ensuring that the assets remain outside his estate for inheritance tax purposes.

3. Maintenance

It is perhaps an inevitable fact of life that arguments over maintenance will often be a feature of a divorce or separation. One of the first questions to be asked (or at least in the forefront of the mind of the parties) is how much am I going to get and how can I get more; alternatively how much am I going to have to pay and how can I pay less. This may sound grasping and cynical but that is to do both parties an injustice. When a marriage breaks down and the spouses are planning to live apart, they will both be acutely aware that it costs more to run two households than one. Furthermore, entertaining, holidays and even vehicles, which would previously have been shared, will now be shared with others and the costs of just carrying on as normal will rocket. Unless there is plenty of money around this is bound to create a bit of a financial strain. If there are ample funds the question of hardship will not arise; it will be a question of sharing out the luxuries. Indeed, it might be more. It may be a wish to have a share of the other spouse's substantial fortune not because of any immediate need to meet expenditure, but to satisfy a different need – that of total financial independence. Sometimes this need is more crudely expressed but the effect is the same. However, in most cases there will simply not be enough money to satisfy the financial requirements of both households. Neither spouse is likely to volunteer hardship just to reduce the hardship of the other spouse. Both will therefore be claiming a share of the same inadequate pot; both will know it and will be anxious lest the other gains an unfair advantage.

That will not always be the case of course. Sometimes one or both parties will be extremely cynical and grasping, activated perhaps by guilt or malice towards the other spouse. I have previously warned against such an approach because you cannot get a quart out of a pint pot, and as you argue over the pot more of the precious contents are spilled. If you want to be vindictive, this is not the way to do it.

To the extent that all these anxieties are the result of ignorance of the rules or an uncertainty about how these rules will operate in the particular case, this chapter may help in understanding how the system works and how to avoid being disadvantaged. The tax implications of any amounts which may be paid are also extremely important because every pound that the husband pays in tax means a pound less is available for the wife; every pound paid in tax by the wife is one pound less she has available to spend. If the tax payable can be reduced it can mean that the wife will receive more even if the husband pays less and this can be a useful way to bridge a gap between conflicting parties. A failure to appreciate the tax rules can lead to a disastrous result.

Until 1988 maintenance payments were tax deductible by the . payer and taxable income in the hands of the recipient. This meant that the awards were somewhat higher in real terms than they are today. The availability of tax relief for the husband gave rise to opportunities for advantage and disadvantage. At its most extreme, prior to 1979/80 when the top tax rate was 98 per cent, a man with a substantial income could pay say £20,000 to his former wife and it would cost him only £400 per annum after tax. The £20,000 would have given rise to tax in the hands of the wife but the rate of tax would have been very much lower with the result that the simple act of transferring income from husband to wife meant that a substantial tax saving arose which they could both enjoy. Even when tax rates were reduced to 60 per cent in 1979 and later to 40 per cent, the scope for tax saving was considerable. But what if the conditions for tax relief were not satisfied? This could and did result in a husband paying maintenance to his wife of an amount greater than his income. I have already referred to one occasion when a husband had agreed to pay 50 per cent of his income to his former wife which he regarded as a reasonable deal. However, because of the way the payments were arranged, they did not qualify for tax relief and because the tax rate was 75 per cent, his income after tax was therefore nowhere near enough to pay the maintenance. Obviously this was an impossible situation and something had to be done; the wife simply could not resist a change in the arrangements. However, the position might not have been so starkly unacceptable. What if the husband had agreed to pay one-third of his income to his former wife and the tax rate was only 40 per cent? The effect would be:

Income	100
Tax at 40%	40
Net income	60
Less: maintenance to wife	33
Amount left for husband	27

Instead of paying his wife one-third of his income he is actually paying her 55 per cent of his net income which is a great deal more than he had in mind. Under these circumstances it may be that the wife would be disinclined to be helpful because the situation may not be so bad as to be insupportable. In any event, he would be at the mercy of his wife.

However, all this came to an end in the Finance Act 1988 which scrapped tax relief for maintenance payments. Since 1988 maintenance payments are not tax deductible from the income of the payer nor are they taxable in the hands of the recipient. This would have been unfair to those who had already entered into obligations for maintenance and there is some continuing tax relief of a modest amount for those with existing commitments. Before dealing with the tax implications, it is necessary to look at the principles behind the entitlement and obligations to maintenance and how it will be determined.

How maintenance is determined

It should be appreciated that the principles and guidelines adopted for all kinds of financial provision were largely developed before 1988 when maintenance was taxed in the hands of the recipient.

Accordingly the awards would have been higher than would normally arise after 1988 because the recipient will keep all the money and not have to send some of it off to the Inland Revenue. Similarly if the husband is not obtaining a tax deduction for the maintenance paid, he will not be able to afford to pay anything like as much. This is a very important consideration to be borne in mind. For the same reasons it is helpful in making a sensible judgement about the maintenance to express it in terms of an equivalent gross amount. After all, that is how people refer to incomes and how comparisons are made even by judges. If maintenance of £1,200 per month is being suggested it would be more easily understood if it were expressed as equal to a gross salary of £20,000 p.a. This figure can then be compared with average earnings or the earnings of a particular employment to judge whether it is adequate to live on.

Ancillary relief

Remember this – it means maintenance; it is money or assets which the court will order to be paid or transferred to the wife to meet her living expenses. It can take the form of:

a) Periodical payments – that is maintenance payments weekly or monthly, secured or unsecured;
b) A lump sum;
c) A settlement of property;
d) A variation of an existing antenuptial or post-nuptial settlement made on the parties to the marriage;
e) A property adjustment order – that is the transfer of property to the spouse or the children.

The court has a wide discretion over these orders and will always look at the particular merits of each case. There are various guidelines about the matters to be considered, but the first point which is of paramount importance is the welfare of the children. Everything comes second to the welfare of the children and unless you appreciate the overwhelming importance of the child's interests, you will be in for a disappointment. The court's duty in connection with financial provision is set out in the Matrimonial Causes Act 1973 and so that you may see the comprehensive nature of their approach, the following are the matters which the court is obliged to consider:

a) The income, earning capacity, property and other financial resources of the parties at the time, or in the foreseeable future, including an increase in the earning capacity which it would be reasonable for them to take steps to acquire. This would for example cover the position where a spouse is not working or attempting to find work or is only working part-time when full-time work is available.
b) The financial needs, obligations and responsibilities of each party at the time and in the foreseeable future. This would cover for example the possibility of inheritance, pension rights and the maturity of endowment policies in due course as well as the property and income of a cohabitee or new spouse.
c) The standard of living enjoyed by the family before the breakdown of the marriage.
d) The age of each party and the duration of the marriage.
e) Any physical or mental disability of either party.
f) The contributions made by each party to the welfare of the family including any contribution by looking after the home or caring for the family.
g) The conduct of the parties.
h) The value of any benefit (a pension, for example) which one party will lose by reason of the divorce.

The court will take all these points into consideration in every case. It may seem rather obvious to say that the property and the earning capacity of both spouses will be taken into account when determining the level and type of financial provision to be ordered. So it is, but it is still important and you should not forget foreseeable changes in resources. If the husband is in an occupation which pays well but is short-lived, such as a footballer or a disc jockey, the fact that higher earnings will arise at an early age must be taken into account. Similarly if the wife has aged parents who are likely to leave her a sizeable amount of money before too long this should not be overlooked. These factors might not affect the amount of any order but they may affect the type of order. For example in the case of the wife with expectations of inheritance, a lump sum award of maintenance might not be appropriate. Such an order would deprive the husband of any opportunity to apply for a variation in his maintenance obligations by reason of the decreased needs of his wife. Once paid, the lump sum could not be recovered. Periodical payments to maintain the wife at a proper level would be much more desirable because they would be capable of adjustment downwards if her financial circumstances were subsequently to improve.

The needs and obligations of the parties are obviously important and bear in mind that these needs must be judged by reference to the standard of living which was enjoyed by the couple before the breakdown of the marriage. Ideally the court would want to put the parties in the same financial position as they would have been without the divorce, but this is rarely possible – most of the time there is simply not enough money. It is the same old story; a conflict over how to slice up the cake.

Those with a cynical disposition may take the view that when the marriage is on the rocks and they fear a divorce may be inevitable, they might do well to upgrade their standard of living. The husband will know that details of his spending habits will all come out in due course so maybe more regular visits to the tailor, a more expensive club, a more prestigious car and possibly some expensive hobbies like flying, hunting or motor racing would not go amiss. For the poor chap to have to give up his hobbies, his club, and to downgrade his BMW or worse would be awful. He would recognize the need to provide adequately for this former wife but to go further than that would obviously be overwhelming hardship.

The wife on the other hand may be of the same mind. Her hairdresser may suddenly be very busy, her dressmaker might have a few more commissions than usual (if she does not have a dressmaker, perhaps she ought to get one pronto), regular lunches with her friends and regular attendance at her health club as well as a full programme of theatre, opera, galleries and museums plus of course Ascot and Wimbledon ought to be arranged. All these things show the lifestyle to which she has been accustomed (all of which require the appropriate dress and grooming), and it would be humiliating for her to slip below this standard.

The risk of course is that they both spend so much money to enhance their lifestyle that there would be nothing left to share out.

The above obviously represents an extreme view but the underlying point is sound and should not be disregarded. But remember that it will do no good if the circumstances have changed. A wife or husband may have been used to an extravagant standard of living while their assets were substantial and Lloyd's was paying them fat cheques each year. If those cheques have stopped and their assets have been depleted by Lloyd's calls, attempts to cling to the earlier lifestyle will do them no good at all.

Where the spouses have a joint bank account which they are both able to use under their own signature, they may regard it as an unacceptable risk that the other could empty the account without notice. It would therefore be a wise precaution to close the account and divide it equally between the parties – except that it may not be possible to do so if they do not agree on the division. There are complex rules about the ownership of the contents of a joint account and assets purchased out of funds contained within it but there remains an assumption of equality; furthermore, on the death of one the other would become entitled to the whole of the balance automatically. If there are substantial funds in the account this is not a point which can be overlooked. It must be dealt with urgently.

When it comes to calculating the wife's needs, these will inevitably be determined by reference to her spending pattern during the period of separation. Where the amounts at stake are significant, that is to say that the funds are available to the husband for the payment of maintenance, it may not be in her interests to adopt a frugal lifestyle during this period. That will be her instinct of course. She will not know how much she will get so she will probably take great care. This could seriously backfire. If she comes to court claiming that she needs £50,000 per year to live on but has to admit that during the last twelve months she has made do with £15,000, an inevitable conclusion will be drawn. It may not be fair, nor will it be the whole picture, but it will be inevitable. If on the other hand she has consistently spent £50,000 during the course of the year and has a complete breakdown of every penny, is it likely that the court would end up giving her only £15,000 a year as maintenance? It might, but common sense dictates that she might do a whole lot better. A balance has to be struck and reasonableness is what really matters. So it is no good claiming that you need £5,000 per month to live on if your husband simply cannot pay it – he may only earn £6,000 which after tax would come down to approximately £4,000. By going for £5,000 you look unreasonable, grasping and generally unworthy of sympathy. By going for the absolute maximum he could possibly afford to pay, while showing that this is a serious sacrifice by reference to your real needs, you obviously will do a lot better.

The ages of the parties and the duration of the marriage will also be significant. This point is most acute where the marriage is very short. There is a general reluctance to place the same degree of financial obligation on the husband of a short childless marriage as there would be on the husband of a long marriage particularly where the wife has devoted herself to bringing up the children. With a short marriage it is much more likely that a clean break will be ordered with little or no maintenance, perhaps just a modest lump sum so that each can go their own way with a minimum of fuss. It is expected that the wife will get a job to support herself in these circumstances and her prospects of employment will also have to be taken into account.

Conduct is less significant than it used to be in deciding the amount of any awards; there is not the same shock horror of adultery or desertion which requires the wronged party to be compensated by an appropriate financial award. However, it may well affect the nature of the maintenance order. An order for periodical payments will cease on the death or remarriage of the payee so if the wife's misconduct has involved cohabitation with a third party in a stable relationship, it would not be too sensible to agree to a lump sum which would not be repayable in the event of marriage. Periodical payments would be much more sensible although different considerations might apply if the cohabitation is with another individual of the same sex.

The fact that the other partner is in a stable relationship with a third party might also affect the amount payable because the contribution of the cohabitee is a factor to be taken into account when assessing her needs. In fact it applies both ways. If the husband and wife both have new partners the court will invariably look at the reality of the situation to judge the real needs of the parties and what funds are available to meet them. A husband who remarries and takes on a responsibility for stepchildren and a substantial new mortgage will simply not be in a position to afford to pay very much to his former wife and children. That may not be fair on them, indeed it is not fair on anybody, because there may simply not be enough money to provide adequately for both families. The answer is that the husband should not have taken on these additional responsibilities which he cannot afford. However, the fact is that he has done so and the court has to deal with that situation. In these cases the first wife should make quite sure that she obtains an order for periodical payments, even if it is only in a nominal sum, so that if circumstances change she can apply to the court for it to be varied. Other aspects such as the possibility of the cohabitant of either party being made to contribute financially to the maintenance of the former spouse are dealt with in Chapter 10.

Some spouses can be very devious and can attempt to conceal or destroy evidence of their wealth. If there is any danger of assets being dealt with in a manner which would adversely affect the effectiveness of any order, precautionary action can be taken. The court has a wide power to defeat attempts to frustrate its orders – for example by transferring assets into a trust or company situated outside the jurisdiction or the sale of assets at an under value to a friend or family member. Dispositions can be set aside, transfers can be restored and the spouse can even be imprisoned. The court has wide powers at its disposal to ensure that its orders are complied with and you have to be very clever indeed (or very foolish) if this is a course of action you intend to follow. If discovered, not only will your efforts be unsuccessful, you can expect no sympathy and probably a penal award against you.

A Mareva injunction can be sought to prevent assets being removed from the jurisdiction and an Anton Piller order can be sought to search premises and seize documents. These orders are extremely invasive of the privacy of the other spouse and will not be given lightly. To be effective they obviously have to be made on the application of only one spouse without the knowledge of the other – otherwise they would obviously be ineffective. The order will only be given where a good case can be made out that there is real danger of improper conduct by the other side and an undertaking will need to be given to pay compensation if damage is suffered as a result of the order being made.

These orders are of general application and do not apply specifically to matrimonial cases. There is a further avenue of opportunity in matrimonial cases which is much less draconian and accordingly requires a much lower standard of proof. Where a spouse can show that she has a claim for financial relief and the other spouse is about to do something which would have the effect of defeating her claim, it will be presumed that this would be the husband's intention enabling the court to make an appropriate order to protect the assets. Where assets have been spirited away, perhaps by transferring them into the name of a friend, the court can set aside the disposition if it took place less than three years before the application.

Where the husband is, or appears to be, insolvent and therefore unable to meet any award which may be ordered by the court, different considerations apply and these are explained in detail in Chapter 8.

Maintenance pending suit

The need for maintenance is likely to arise long before the divorce is finally ordered. The wife and children could be seriously disadvantaged, indeed destitute, by simply dragging out the proceedings. It is therefore possible to seek an order for maintenance pending suit as an interim measure. The court will be in difficulty here because it would not want to order amounts to be paid which are greater than the final order is likely to be because that would obviously be unfair to the husband; it would also be unfair on the wife by falsely inflating her expectations. But at this early stage, insufficient information will be available to the court to determine what the final outcome is likely to be so the court will inevitably err on the low side. In the end the final order can be backdated to the date of the original petition so that the wife will not necessarily lose out, but there could be a significant cash flow detriment in the meantime.

Interim payments

Do not confuse maintenance pending suit with interim periodical payments. Maintenance pending suit is intended to assist the spouse during the period before the court has considered the position; interim payments are made by the court when it has power to order periodical payments but has not yet made up its mind about the amount.

Secured maintenance

We have looked at the matters which will be considered in assessing the amount of maintenance to be paid but there is another important feature: will it actually be paid? It is one thing having a court order in your favour, it is quite another to be sure of getting the money. One simple means of ensuring that the payments continue is to have secured maintenance, that is, secured by a deposit out of which the maintenance is paid, or secured by a charge on an asset which can be used to meet the obligation to make the payments if for any reason they cease. From the wife's point of view secured maintenance is extremely attractive because it is obviously much safer. It will last longer than unsecured maintenance because it does not stop on the death of the husband. What is more it will take priority over any creditors in the event of the husband's bankruptcy. The tax implications of secured maintenance are not at all straightforward and will have an important influence on whether either of the parties wants the maintenance to be secured. This is dealt with in more detail below.

One-third rule

In any discussion about maintenance the one-third rule will not take long to arise. To say that the one-third rule is of uncertain application is to overstate the position considerably. Everybody seems to have a different idea. It started life in a case called Wachtel v. Wachtel in 1973 and was based on the premise that one-third of the combined assets of the parties should be the starting point for the division between husband and wife. One might start with the proposition that the assets of the parties should be divided equally between them. That is fair enough if both brought nothing to the marriage and have worked jointly in the enhancement of the family wealth. But it is less satisfactory where a wealthy man marries a poor wife or vice versa. Where the husband's efforts at work create wealth while his wife cares for the home and family it can be strongly argued that he brings the increased wealth to the marriage to be shared equally. If on the divorce it is suggested that the capital assets be divided equally, in the absence of special factors, this would obviously make a lot of sense. However, that is not what is often suggested. Those who argue for an equal division also suggest that the income should be divided equally as well. That is where the logic breaks down because in that case the wife is saying that not only does she want half the existing capital, but she wants half of the continuing income long after the marriage has ceased. The courts have suggested that she may have a case for half the income or half the capital, but not both. Such a claim also fails to take into account that the husband may take a new partner and have a second family to whom he will also be financially responsible. It is therefore no surprise that the courts developed a broad reconciliation between the present and future assets with one-third of the capital and one-third of the joint income. The calculation is not difficult. If we assume the husband earns £45,000 and the wife earns £15,000 it would go like this:

Husband's income	£45,000
Wife's income	£15,000
	£60,000
One-third thereof	£20,000
Less wife's income	£15,000
Maintenance to wife	**£5,000**

That was all very well when the husband received an income tax deduction for his maintenance payments and the wife paid tax on what she received. But now with neither party getting a tax deduction for the payments or paying tax on receipts, the figures go seriously awry. The calculation ought to be done on a net of tax basis so as to preserve the principle – otherwise it goes all wrong. If we revise the figures used above on to a net basis, the maintenance becomes:

Husband	£45,000	=	33,000 (net of tax)
Wife	£15,000	=	12,000 (net of tax)
	£45,000		
One-third thereof	15,000		
Less wife's income	12,000		
Maintenance to wife	**3,000**		

For the husband to pay £5,000 net would be equal to a gross amount of £6,666 which is more than twice as much as would have been the expectation under the order.

It is necessary to appreciate that certain deductions are allowable from the income to arrive at the net income for the purposes of this calculation, whether it is done before tax or after tax. Such expenditure as National Insurance contributions, compulsory pension payments, travelling expenses to and from work and in particular any amounts payable to the children for their education can be deducted. Where the husband is self-employed there will be different arguments. The husband will want to have the assessment of his income based on his tax assessment because that will be after deduction of all the expenses his accountant can possibly claim. Why, he will say, should the wife challenge a deduction if it has been agreed by the Inland Revenue of all people – they are not exactly famous for their generosity in allowing deductions. On the other hand, the wife may argue that some of his expenses will be related to his ordinary cost of living such as light and heat at home, telephone and motor expenses and will contain an element of fixed costs which the husband would have had to pay anyway.

The one-third rule has come under increasing criticism over the years and is now a rule of thumb which nobody adheres to with any great conviction. The change in the tax rules diminishes its usefulness even further. It is perhaps best to treat it as it was originally intended, just as a starting point, never having gained universal acceptance as a tariff. It could be that an inflexible one-third rule would have given the wife much more than she would ever have needed in big money cases and it had to be disregarded. One lasting principle can perhaps be discerned, which is that the entitlement of the wife should not exceed her own needs during her lifetime; there is no need for the husband to contribute to, or satisfy, her testamentary wishes. It may be this thinking which led to the development of the Duxbury calculation which is explained in more detail in connection with lump sums.

Clean break

The clean break has become an important feature in divorce proceedings, the objective being for there to be a once and for all settlement, a lump sum or transfer of property with no periodical payments, enabling the parties to put the past behind them and to begin a new life which is not overshadowed by the earlier relationship, at least in financial terms. This overshadowing can take two forms; the first is the continuing connection between the parties which periodical payments inevitably involve; the second is the possibility of the wife coming back for more money if she sees her husband prospering – or conversely of the husband applying for a downwards variation in his maintenance obligations because he has fallen on hard times. It is unclear whether the wife's rights to periodical payments can be taken away without her consent although in practice this seems to be the case.

The most obvious case where a clean break is entirely appropriate is a short childless marriage. In such a case, a lump sum or property transfer will invariably be made and the parties will go their separate ways.

However, this is not always the case. A clean break would certainly be inappropriate where there are children – you cannot have a clean break from your children – and the introduction of the Child Support Act 1991 has caused clean-break settlements to be fraught with difficulty – and positive danger for the husband. This is explained in more detail in Chapter 4. In cases where the marriage had been of long duration, and the wife had not been employed for many years, the lump sum would have to be very large and possibly unaffordable to make her financially independent. Where resources are insufficient, obviously a clean break is not possible and periodical payments are the only answer.

Lump sums

There is a great deal to be said for lump sums on both sides; these are the arguments in favour of a clean break which unfortunately is not usually possible. While the court will consider a lump sum in every case, there has to be capital out of which a lump sum can be paid. No order for a lump sum can be made if there are inadequate resources or if it would cripple the husband's earning power. Nor is it likely that a lump sum order will be made in favour of a child, despite the court's ability to do so. Children do not have any special claim on their parents' money and any award will only be made in cases where the child suffers from some disability or there are other reasons why it has special needs.

Where there are sufficient capital assets to allow a lump sum to be paid this is likely to be eagerly sought by the wife who will gain an extra layer of financial security; a lump sum is protection against the possible decline in her husband's fortunes, bankruptcy or even death. Many a wife has been left with nothing because the maintenance commitment became impossible as a result of her husband's insolvency. On the other hand it can also be attractive to the husband, particularly if he expects his financial situation to improve.

However, the most compelling reason is that he can put this obligation behind him leaving himself free to develop his business and his life without the anxiety that however successful he is, his ex-wife will always be looking over his shoulder. With this coincidence of interest in support of a lump sum the parties will often have no difficulty at all in reaching agreement that a lump sum ought to be paid. Unfortunately the agreement is likely to be only in principle; the disagreement, as always, will be on how much the lump sum should be. There may be no reconciliation to this disagreement although one possibility would be for the lump sum to be paid in instalments, thereby enabling the parties to obtain the advantage of a lump sum where capital may not be readily available. However this is unlikely to be attractive in practice. A lump sum payable by instalments looks awfully like a periodical payment and is subject to the same risks; the husband might stop paying for one reason or another – disaffection or insolvency, for example. The protection sought by the wife by the provision of a lump sum may simply not exist. Worse still, the court does not have power to vary a lump sum award. If the husband's financial situation improves the wife cannot apply for an increase in payments, but she risks losing out if his financial situation deteriorates. As far as the husband is concerned he is committed to this obligation and although it cannot go up, it cannot go down either, short of insolvency.

The solution for the wife is for the lump sum payable by instalments to be accompanied by a nominal periodical payments order, say £5 per annum, which would be capable of variation upwards if the husband's finances improve. This however is hardly compatible with a clean break which would have been the idea behind the lump sum order in the first place – nor is it likely to find favour with the husband who is stuck with the equivalent of an upwards only review.

Nevertheless where a lump sum is desirable by both parties and payment by instalments is the only available means of payment, these disadvantages can be overcome by placing appropriate conditions on the provision of the lump sum or the provision of security.

Another alternative would be a contingent lump sum order, that is one which becomes payable on the happening of a future event such as the sale of an asset or the receipt of a lump sum from a pension scheme. As explained in Chapter 6 there are some difficulties with this type of order in practical terms, and in cases of army and air force personnel there are statutory prohibitions against making awards from service pensions which need to be overcome.

Where the matrimonial home is the only capital asset and the wife stays in occupation, a lump sum would obviously be inappropriate but if she leaves and he stays, it is more probable that the wife will be allowed a lump sum based on the value of the property. The amount is likely to be as much as the husband can raise by a further mortgage on the house without crippling him financially.

However it may be of interest to know that in a recent survey of big money cases the lump sum awards were all around 30 per cent of the assets where the marriage had been well established without any significant variation on the length of the marriage. In a short marriage a lump sum is much more likely to arise because of the additional desirability of a clean break. However, the amount of the lump sum will be nowhere near the level which would apply to a long-standing wife but would merely be sufficient for her to get on her feet again. At the other end of the spectrum, where the lump sum award is likely to be fairly small, you should be careful to take into account the £2,500 exemption limit from the legal aid charge and the £3,000 limit which applies for the purposes of income support.

Sometimes it is the husband who seeks the lump sum from the wife, but these cases are far less common. Where the assets originate from the husband and were put into the wife's ownership or perhaps assets belonging to the wife were developed and enhanced in value by the husband, a lump sum becomes appropriate. Where the wife's assets are much greater than those of the husband it may be appropriate for him to be provided with a suitable home so that he can accommodate the children on visits, but this will be rare except where substantial sums are involved; in those cases batteries of lawyers will be considering matters way beyond the scope of this book.

Duxbury calculations

The Duxbury calculation is a means of calculating the lump sum and is found by working back from a figure of periodical payments. The idea is that a lump sum be calculated which will be enough to meet the requirements of the wife for the rest of her life on the basis that she draws capital as well as income. In other words it is a lump sum sufficient to provide an annuity. However, it is more than a simple annuity because it takes into account future changes in circumstances, reduced needs as the children grow up and the possibility of moving to a smaller house. The calculations are complex and you do not need to worry about them because the accountants or lawyers will have to provide the figures based on assessments of investment yields, inflation, life expectancy and tax. But first you have to decide how much is needed year by year on which to live – so we are back to a calculation of periodical payments.

Variation of orders

It is possible for an application to be made to vary an existing order. Periodical payment orders can be varied by the court, but not transfers of property or lump sums (except where they are being paid by instalments) so you need to be very careful about the implications before you agree to a consent order which effects a clean break with a transfer of property or lump sum with no periodical payments. The court cannot extinguish a charge in favour of the husband on the transfer of the matrimonial home to the wife but it is possible to accelerate the termination of a Mesher order if the purpose has already been fulfilled – that is, the children have already left home.

Mesher orders have a lot going for them with the clean-break principle and the obvious security for the wife, but if circumstances change she may kick herself that she did not have some periodical payments which could be revised. A nominal periodical payments order of, for example, £5 per annum would solve the problem because if necessary it can be varied by the court to something more substantial.

This may be attractive to the wife because it gives her all the advantages of a clean-break order without any of the disadvantages. Conversely it is highly unattractive to the husband. He gets no advantages whatsoever from it. He has to fork out a lump sum for the clean-break settlement but it is not a clean break at all because she can still come back for more by varying the periodical payments order. In normal cases the husband and wife are on an equal footing with periodical payments; each can go back to the court for a variation if circumstances change. The husband can seek a reduction if his financial circumstances deteriorate and although there is nothing to prevent a husband doing so with a nominal payments order, it is hardly going to do him any good. It is a one-way adjustment which is hardly fair on him.

When looking at an application to vary the periodical payments order, the court will look at all the original matters which existed at the time of the original order to see what has changed; however it does not have to look only at the situation since that date; it can look at the whole thing again if that will be more appropriate. The court also has power to bring the periodical payments to an end or to provide a time limit on future payments.

Repeat applications

Once the court has considered the position and made an order for an ancillary relief it cannot entertain another application for the same type of ancillary relief for the same spouse. All it can do is vary an order which has already been made. So once an application is dismissed, that is the end of that. If the court therefore decides that a transfer of property should be made and all other claims should be dismissed, those dismissed claims cannot be revived. Unfortunately, as we have seen, a transfer of property order cannot be varied either. Alternatively, if an application for ancillary relief is granted at a low level and a lump sum application is dismissed through want of assets, the fact that the husband later acquires substantial assets which would otherwise have enabled a lump sum to have been paid, that cannot be dealt with. An increase in the periodical payments would be the best that could be done.

Separation agreements

It is open to the parties not to institute divorce or other proceedings but simply to agree to live apart under a separation agreement. This would be a contract, enforceable just like any business contract and would cover the payment of maintenance, the distribution of the family property and all the arrangements for the children. The agreement does not have to be in writing, but unless there is some written document, it may be difficult to prove it in the event of a dispute.

The parties cannot exclude the jurisdiction of the courts from the regulation of their affairs and they should take care that they do not even try to do so. Not only would it be ineffective but it is likely to render the entire agreement void which may be seriously disadvantageous for one side.

A separation agreement has a number of advantages similar to those which apply to a decree of judicial separation; the parties remain married although their respective obligations to live together are terminated. It is a halfway house which the parties may use to regularize their affairs while they are deciding what they will do in the future. A separation agreement is just as formal in effect and equally binding as a decree of judicial separation, but because it does not involve the court, being just an agreement between the parties, it seems less formal and therefore easier to arrange.

Any transfer of property made under a separation agreement will remain exempt from inheritance tax by reason of the spouse exemption but the capital gains tax exemption for transfers between spouses will not apply after the end of the tax year in which the separation takes place. A separation is therefore a good opportunity to effect transfers of property while the parties are still married and living together (or at least if they can do so before the end of the year of assessment) so that the exemption can be preserved.

Collection and enforcement

It is one thing getting an order from the court but that does not pay the bills; you need to ensure you get the money. The wife who has been awarded a periodical payments order on a secured basis will have few problems – at least in ensuring that the periodical payments are made. If they stop she has a ready-made security which she can enforce without delay; that is the security. Unfortunately, secured maintenance is rarely ordered and there are some serious adverse tax implications which means that most maintenance will be unsecured. Therefore the wife may be in a state of continual anxiety about whether or not her husband will continue to make the payments.

Child support payments made through the Child Support Agency will be collected by the Agency and they are likely to be pretty effective at doing so, although with a growing work load, the enforcement process may start to take rather longer than it should. Spousal maintenance will be enforced just like any other debt although there are plans for it to be collectable by the CSA after 1996. It also retains the same disadvantage that it depends upon the ability to pay; you cannot sue a man who has no income or assets – at least you can try and it will cost you a great deal in professional fees but you will still not get the money. The threat of committal to prison for non-payment is by far the most effective course but naturally the courts are rather reluctant to make such an order. Although the threat may be highly effective, if he does not pay and goes to prison, the maintenance will certainly not be paid and it may damage the chances of it being paid in the future. It must therefore be shown to the satisfaction of the court that the husband has the money to pay the maintenance and is wilfully refusing to do so. In effect he is defying a court order to make periodical payments; defying court orders invariably carries with it the risk of prison.

This is the extreme solution but it does nobody any good to be in dispute over unpaid maintenance. It is much better for the payments to continue. One way of doing this is by an attachment of earnings order so that the maintenance is deducted each month from the husband's salary and paid over to the court rather in the way that tax is deducted from earnings and paid over to the Inland Revenue. An attachment of earnings order in connection with maintenance does not require the debtor's consent; however, it does have the particular difficulty that if the husband is not employed or if he is self-employed there is nothing to which an attachment of earnings order can attach itself.

Another alternative is to seek a warrant of execution which is the technical way of saying that you send the bailiffs in. That can be pretty effective too, because bailiffs tend to be rather purposeful gentlemen and nobody will want his goods seized by the bailiff even if those goods are of little value.

There is also a garnishee order which enables the wife to apply to any third party who owes money to her husband (such as a bank, assuming his account is in credit) to pay the money direct to her. This can be a surprisingly effective remedy and very easy to obtain. However there is a general rule that the court will only enforce arrears to periodical payments up to twelve months.

When the default is the failure to pay a lump sum or transfer property, a charging order can be made against one of the husband's assets immediately followed by an order for it to be sold so that the lump sum can be paid out of the sale proceeds. In the case of a transfer of property order, the court can itself execute the relevant documentation if necessary. Again this is highly effective, not necessarily in realizing the assets but in encouraging the husband to comply because he can see exactly what will happen if he does not.

Why bother?

You may say that you do not need all this. The court has power to do this and discretion to do that; what you want is to know how it is going to end up. However, that is to overlook an important tactical position. If you understand how the court will approach the problem and the sort of basis upon which any award will be made, and more importantly the things which the court will certainly not do, you are in a good position to develop a plan to put the other side at a disadvantage. You can suggest a compromise. If it is done skilfully, you can make the suggested compromise heavily weighted in your favour but nevertheless tempting, particularly when combined with a Calderbank letter, and unnerve the other into agreement. Think of their position. Here is an offer which although not in the least generous, is just about at the limits of what the court would order – or at least even if the whole package may be a bit much it might be difficult to say which part, if any, the court would disagree with. If you reject it, you risk ending up in the same place anyway and meeting all the future costs of both sides.

So by taking note of the above points you can put yourself in a good position to structure the settlement on your terms instead of just carrying on in a vacuum – being carried along by the advisers without necessarily having any particular plan. However, there is one further aspect which you must always take into account and that is tax.

Taxation of maintenance

Various references have been made above to the need to consider the tax position when considering claims for ancillary relief and the horrors that can befall you if the tax implications are overlooked. It has been explained that before 1988, maintenance payments were tax deductible by the payer and were taxable income in the hands of the recipient. In March 1988 the position changed so that the payments were no longer tax deductible and the recipient was no longer taxable on the income. This applies also to payments made direct to a child and to maintenance payments arising outside the United Kingdom. That is the general rule but, as always with tax matters, there are some exceptions.

Where the maintenance is paid under a court order or written agreement from one spouse to the other, the payer will be entitled to an allowance for the payments but this is limited to £1,720, the amount of the married couple's allowance. Where the amounts paid are less, the allowance is less. However, this is just a relief to the payer; it has no effect on the recipient for whom the maintenance remains tax free. The payments are made gross, without any tax deduction, and are not taxable in the hands of the recipient. It must be noted that voluntary payments or those under a binding oral agreement will not qualify for this relief which requires the payments to be made under a written agreement or court order. Although the relief is very modest you might as well have it, particularly as all it needs is for the payments you make to be enshrined in a written document.

Also, there is no relief in respect of payments made direct to the child. This is really a trap because payments made to the other spouse specifically for the benefit of the child will qualify for the relief and will usually amount to the same thing. Furthermore, the relief stops on remarriage of the recipient, even if the obligation to pay continues. However, this problem will not arise where the payment is made under a maintenance assessment in respect of the child and is collected by the Child Support Agency. In that case the payments for the child will count as qualifying maintenance payments for the purposes of the relief.

For those who are in the unfortunate position of having to pay maintenance to more than one former or separated spouse, there is only one such allowance; you do not get a separate allowance in respect of each set of maintenance payments.

It is important, however, not to get carried away because this relief is not worth very much. The maximum allowance is £1,720 per annum and although it was given at the payer's marginal rate of tax up to 6 April 1994, it was given only at the 20 per cent rate of tax for 1994/95 and at only 15 per cent for 1995/96. £1,720 at 15 per cent is therefore worth only £258 per annum at best so it is not worth getting too excited about.

Existing obligations

The new system for the taxation of maintenance payments came into force on 15 March 1988 and of course there are people who were already paying maintenance at that date under the old rules. The court orders were made on the basis of the law at the time, and it would therefore be unfair to change the rules for those existing obligations. Accordingly, there are some special provisions for those who are in this situation so that they are not unfairly treated – or at least not too unfairly. What happens is that those who were making periodical payments before 15 March 1988 will continue to obtain a tax deduction for maintenance payments even after that date – but the amount allowed will be pegged to the amount paid in the year ended 5 April 1989.

In some cases it may be more advantageous for the payer to be subject to the new rules and not to the old system, an election can be made for this treatment within twelve months of the end of the tax year to which the election relates. The effect of this election is that the maintenance becomes tax free in the hands of the recipient and the payer will be entitled only to a deduction of £1,720 (or such lower amount as may be paid) at the appropriate rate of tax. This may not seem to be particularly advantageous but an example will show where the benefit lies:

Adam was paying Eve £1,500 per annum under a court order on 6 April 1986. This was increased to £1,800 on 6 April 1988 and to £3,000 on 6 April 1994. Adam is entitled to tax relief on the maintenance paid under the old system despite the introduction of the new rules but his relief is pegged to the amount of maintenance paid in 1988/89 which was £1,800. The extra amounts he now pays do not qualify for any relief. Adam could make an election for his maintenance payments to be treated as falling within the new rules. In that way he would receive tax relief for only £1,720 (instead of £1,800) at the lower rates of tax, but Eve would not be liable to tax on any of the maintenance payments received. Her net income would thereby be significantly increased and she may well feel disposed to share some of this advantage with Adam – after all, it is the election he made that created her advantage.

Secured maintenance: tax implications

The tax implications of secured maintenance are entirely different. Secured maintenance can take a number of forms but the normal arrangement would be for the husband to transfer assets to trustees to hold on trust to pay an amount equal to the maintenance to the wife and any surplus to him. When the obligation for maintenance ceases, the assets are returned to the husband. However, it could be arranged differently; the assets transferred to the trustees could give rise to no income and they could be held by the trustees simply as security to which the wife could look in the event that her husband defaults on his payments.

These two types of secured maintenance have very different tax implications. In the first, although the maintenance is paid out of the trust fund, the amounts paid to the wife are taxable in her hands despite the fact that maintenance is not normally chargeable to tax. Similarly, that amount of income being used to satisfy the maintenance obligations of the husband means that he effectively receives tax relief for the payments. This has the effect of preserving the pre-1988 position as far as tax relief is concerned and can be of considerable benefit to the spouses. For example, if the maintenance payable to the wife is £25,000 per annum and it is arranged by secured maintenance in this manner, the tax payable by the wife would be:

Wife's income		£25,000
Personal allowance	£3,525	
Additional personal allowance	£1,720	£5,245
		£19,755
£3,200 at 20%		£640
£16,555 at 25%		£4,139
		£4,779

But assuming he is a higher rate taxpayer, the husband will be obtaining tax relief at 40 per cent on the whole £25,000 because without these arrangements that £25,000 would have been taxed as income in his hands at 40 per cent – that is a tax saving of £10,000. So by arranging matters in this way there is a tax saving of over £5,000 which can be shared between the parties. This is obviously to everybody's advantage except the Inland Revenue. It is however absolutely essential that in making the order, by consent or other-wise, the precise tax position is understood. If not, and if it were to be assumed that the payments would be free of tax just like ordinary maintenance payments, the wife will find herself with maintenance of £4,779 less than she thought. The husband on the other hand would be delighted to find that his maintenance payments were costing him not £25,000 but only £15,000.

Unfortunately, just to make life difficult, the tax position with the other type of secured maintenance is not the same at all. In that case it is the husband who is paying the maintenance payments and they will be outside the scope of tax, being free of tax in the hands of the recipient and not tax deductible by the husband. This is because the trust containing the security is not making any payment to the wife; it is merely providing security in the event of the husband's default. Any income arising to the trustees of a settlement in these circumstances would be taxable on the husband in the normal way.

The capital gains tax position should not be overlooked because any transfers of assets to trustees, even a trust in which the husband has an interest, will be treated as a sale at market value for capital gains tax purposes. If that gives rise to a capital gain because the assets transferred are worth more than the original cost as adjusted for indexation, capital gains tax will arise in the normal way – unless there is any opportunity to hold over the gain (which is unlikely because a transfer of assets in these circumstances is unlikely to be a gift) or the gain is an exempt gain (for example, if the asset transferred by way of security was an interest in the matrimonial home). Accordingly assets chosen for this purpose should be selected as those which do not give rise to any capital gain – or of course cash, which is not chargeable to capital gains tax anyway. Any gains made by the trustees during the existence of the settlement will be taxed on the husband as his gains. When the trust comes to an end by reason of the obligation for the maintenance ceasing, or for another reason, and the assets are transferred back to the husband, that transfer will itself be regarded as a disposal by the trustees of the assets at market value and again a capital gains tax liability might arise. The only circumstance when this would not arise is if the trust came to an end by the death of the wife. On that event part or all of the trust property would be revalued without any charge to capital gains tax. A fund of cash would have none of these problems.

Unfortunately the inheritance tax position is just as complicated. A transfer of assets to a trust for the purpose of paying maintenance to the wife will not be a transfer of value for inheritance tax purposes even if it would have been a transfer under general principles; that is doubtful anyway because it would not have been set up to confer a gratuitous benefit on any individual – it would have been set up by court order. If the trust comes to an end, for example on the death or remarriage of the wife, the reversion of the trust fund to her husband would ensure that no inheritance tax would arise on that occasion. There is a special exemption from inheritance tax where trust property reverts to the settlor on the death of a beneficiary. However, if the husband were to die first while the trust is in existence and still satisfying the obligations for maintenance, the value of his reversionary interest would form part of his estate and be chargeable to tax. To make matters worse, on the subsequent death of the wife the trust fund would be chargeable as part of her estate because the special exemption would not apply, the settlor being already dead. Even if the maintenance ceases during her lifetime and the trust fund reverts to the estate of her deceased former husband, that would be regarded as a potentially exempt transfer on which inheritance tax would arise if she were to die within seven years. This could have a very unfortunate effect because if she were to die within seven years and the trust fund was worth, say, £150,000, this potentially exempt transfer would become a chargeable transfer to be taken into account in her estate. That would not give rise to any inheritance tax because the £150,000 transfer would be below the level at which inheritance tax is chargeable, but it would substantially erode her nil rate band leaving the remainder of her estate fully chargeable to tax at 40 per cent. Her family might therefore end up paying £60,000 more inheritance tax by reason of this earlier transfer without any recourse to the trust fund to meet the tax.

This catastrophe can be avoided by arranging for the maintenance to be secured by the second of the above alternatives – that is where the trust fund merely contains the security and the husband makes the maintenance payments himself. However, that may not give rise to the tax position desired by the parties.

Quite apart from the tax implications it is rarely possible for the court to make such an order. The whole point is to protect the wife by ensuring that the husband will not default. There are lots of ways of enforcing payment except where the husband has no money or assets. In that case he will be unable to provide the necessary funds for security. If he has got sufficient assets, the chances are he will be able to be pursued if he fails to satisfy the payments – so security would not be necessary. It is really only those cases where the husband has inadequate means to provide the security and there is some danger that he will leave the jurisdiction that secured maintenance has any real relevance.

Lump sums

Lump sums payable to the spouse by way of maintenance either by the court or by agreement between the parties themselves will not be liable to any tax in the hands of the recipient or tax relief by the payer. Capital gains tax will not apply either because cash is not chargeable to capital gains tax. However, a problem arises if the lump sum were to be satisfied in foreign currency. Foreign currency is a chargeable asset for capital gains tax purposes which means that a capital gain could arise on its disposal. The transfer of the foreign currency to the spouse would be a disposal of that foreign currency at market value at the date of the transfer and if the exchange rate had moved significantly since the foreign currency had been acquired, a capital gain could arise:

Adam is ordered to pay Eve a lump sum of US $100,000 to be satisfied out of his US dollar account. The money in the US dollar account had been deposited some time ago on the sale of some US securities. At the time the exchange rate was US $1.76 to the £1 but at the time of the transfer to Eve the dollar was standing at US $1.50 to the £1. The position would therefore be as under:

Cost of dollars on acquisition – 100,000 at 1.76	£56,818
Value of dollars on disposal – 100,000 at 1.50	£66,666
Capital gain	**£9,848**

This is could be an entirely unexpected gain which would be taxable in Adam's hands, arising solely by reason of the currency fluctuations. This situation is obviously best avoided.

As far as inheritance tax is concerned, a lump sum is unlikely to be any kind of transfer because the transfer would not be made with any gratuitous intent but as a result of the court order. Alternatively it would be made by one spouse to the other by way of provision for her maintenance and be exempt on that ground.

School fees

Prior to 5 April 1988 various arrangements were made so that a tax deduction was effectively obtained for school fee payments. The most extreme case concerned a man who lived alone with his children but sought an order through the courts against himself for payment of their school fees. He succeeded in obtaining a tax deduction in this way, but that opportunity was soon removed by a change in the law although it showed the imagination which can and ought to be deployed in matrimonial breakdowns to achieve the best tax position. To the extent that the arrangements had been made before 5 April 1988 and the amounts continue to be paid (although by now they would nearly all have come to an end) some relief may still be available under the transitional provisions for existing obligations. However, there is perhaps an alternative means of obtaining an advantage, which is where the husband's family company or employer makes the payments for him.

Let us assume that Adam is employed by a trading company, Vipers Limited. His employer wants to benefit Adam and enters into a contract with the school which his daughter Evette will attend to provide education for her. The contract is between the school and Vipers Limited; Adam has nothing to do with it. Evette goes to the school, the school sends the bills to Vipers Limited which pays the fees amounting to £6,000. As far as tax is concerned the payment to the school will be regarded as a benefit to Adam and he will be chargeable to tax as if he had received a salary of £6,000. This would cost him £1,500 (assuming he is a basic rate taxpayer) which is obviously a lot better than £6,000. The company would be entitled to a tax deduction for the payments made because they would represent part of Adam's salary package. The advantage to the company is that it would not have to pay National Insurance contributions on the provision of this benefit in kind to Adam and this would save them 10.2 per cent – that is £612. Everybody benefits this way but it is not quite as good as it sounds. If Adam had received a bonus of £6,000, this would have amounted to £4,500 after tax and it would only have cost him a further £1,500 to pay the school fees. This sounds the same but bear in mind the National Insurance contributions saving for the company and there is also a delay in payment of the tax if the company provides a benefit in kind. Instead of the tax being payable under PAYE in the normal fashion it would be payable a year or more later after submission of the various tax returns and this cash flow advantage should not be disregarded.

Foreign divorces and foreign maintenance

Parties to a foreign divorce can apply for financial relief in the United Kingdom but only if one of the parties is domiciled or habitually resident here or has an interest in a United Kingdom property which has been the matrimonial home. The United Kingdom courts will recognize a divorce in a foreign country if either party is a national or habitual resident here. The divorce must have been granted in judicial proceedings which use domicile as a basis for its jurisdiction.

Providing the divorce is recognized in this country as valid, an application for ancillary relief can be made – but don't bank on it; it is only by leave of the court and that will only be given if they think that the English courts are the appropriate forum. They will not think so if the connection of the parties with this country is only temporary or insubstantial or where financial relief could have been sought under the law of another country and no application has been made there without good reason. More practically, they will probably not grant leave if the property in respect of which the order would be made is mainly outside the United Kingdom or if the order may prove to be unenforceable.

The tests are really codified common sense and you should ask yourself – is there any good reason why the English courts should become involved in this case? If they were not to do so, would there be an injustice or real hardship which could not otherwise be remedied?

Assuming the United Kingdom courts accept jurisdiction they will deal with the matter in the same way as an application for ancillary relief in respect of a United Kingdom divorce subject to the same rules and guidelines – although they will be a little constrained if the relevant assets are abroad. Where the court entertains an order by reason only that the matrimonial home is in the United Kingdom their powers are limited and they can only make a property adjustment order in respect of that property or the proceeds of sale – they cannot make a periodical payments order, secured or unsecured.

As far as tax is concerned, maintenance received in this country from abroad will be free of tax in the hands of the recipient just as if the order had been made by a United Kingdom court.

A problem arises in connection with tax relief for payments made under a foreign court order in existence in 1988/89. It will be remembered that the general rule is that maintenance payments in respect of which a payer is entitled to relief during 1988/89 can be continued at that level in subsequent years despite the introduction of the new rules. However, relief for foreign maintenance payments could only have been given against foreign income so if the husband's foreign income is high, the continuity of relief at the same level will be secured. However, if he had no foreign income during 1988/89, the Inland Revenue take the view that there can be no entitlement to relief. There would be an opportunity to elect for treatment under the new system but only if the recipient was resident in the United Kingdom. If not, the payments would not be eligible for treatment as qualifying maintenance payments and no relief would be available at all unless the court order was made in a court in an EC state. In that event relief would be allowed but only up to the £1,720 limit.

It may be however that the payer could still claim the married couple's allowance of £1,720 because if the maintenance payments are the only income of the wife, the husband could reasonably claim that he is continuing to maintain her.

4. Children

The paramount consideration

The existence of children can be the most important feature in divorce proceedings. The court will give their primary attention to considering what is best for the children. They have to – their statutory duty is for first consideration to be given to the welfare of the minor children of the family. Before looking at the money, the court will consider who should have the parental responsibility of the child – that is to say, who will have custody and who will decide the important matters such as schooling, religious upbringing and where they will live. You do not have to be a parent to be given parental responsibility – a relative who is looking after the child on a permanent basis, such as a grandparent, can be given parental responsibility. In many cases these arrangements will be agreed between the parties but that will not necessarily mean the court will agree; it probably will, but you cannot be sure, particularly where there are lots of other implications. Where the parties do not agree, the court will make a determination – but only after they have gone into all the relevant facts, including of course all the unpleasant characteristics of each party which make both of them seem wholly unsuitable as custodians of the child. One wonders sometimes whether it can possibly be in the interest of the child to live with either parent if half what they say about each other is true. All the awful descriptions about the personal habits of the parties are bound to have an effect on the child. However, this chapter is not concerned with these matters but with the financial arrangements which will be made in respect of the child.

Child Support Agency

Before April 1993 the court had power to order maintenance for the child in similar fashion as for the spouse. Not any more. Subject to a transitional period up to April 1997 authority rests entirely in the Child Support Agency by virtue of the Child Support Act 1991. After April 1997 the court will have absolutely nothing to do with it – at least that is the idea. Unfortunately the Child Support Agency has run into a number of problems (growing daily as I write) that it cannot be expected to remain operating in the same way indefinitely.

The Child Support Agency is a government department, part of the Department of Social Security, and the plan is that the CSA determines the child's maintenance requirements and enforces it themselves. They have extensive powers to trace defaulting parents. It was anticipated that this would be the best means of ensuring that parents make proper provision for their children and do not evade their responsibilities leaving the State to support the family. Child maintenance will only be a matter for the courts where the CSA does not have jurisdiction. The CSA is not entirely comprehensive. It applies only:

a) In respect of natural or adopted children – not stepchildren;
b) In respect of maintenance – not for lump sums or property transactions;
c) In respect of children under sixteen, or those under nineteen who are still at school;
d) If the parties are resident in the United Kingdom – if the child or either parent is abroad you must apply to the court;
e) If there is no existing maintenance order.

The courts will retain jurisdiction in those areas where the CSA does not apply and in particular in respect of:

a) Children of wealthy parents where maintenance above the CSA limits would be appropriate;
b) School fees;
c) The additional needs of disabled children.

The CSA started life as a system to deal only with claimants who were on benefit, and it was intended to extend it to everybody; this idea has now been deferred for the foreseeable future. Even at the moment the overwhelming amount of work seems inevitably to mean that almost every assessment they make is wrong but there is no mechanism for the court to put it right. You do not have to wait until the divorce before you make an application to the CSA for maintenance for the child. You can make an application immediately upon separation.

It may be tempting if there is an existing maintenance order to apply to have that award set aside so that the CSA can take over the case and possibly award a higher amount of support for the child. That is a high risk. You should not even consider this without legal advice because you could find yourself in a limbo without any money coming in and with a need to commence court proceedings – and not a lot of sympathy. Much better to apply for a variation. An application can be made by the parent or person with care of the child – so that could be a grandparent if they are looking after the children permanently.

The CSA has the right to reopen clean-break orders to obtain more money for the children from the absent parent. This is highly controversial but the reasoning is that there is a continuing responsibility to the children which cannot be ousted by a clean-break order. It follows the principle that you cannot have a clean break from your children. Where a husband has made a generous capital settlement instead of generous periodical payments for the spouse and child, he could be financially undone. The power to disregard capital provision has recently been curtailed but it remains highly unsatisfactory because it is based on expediency without even any attempt to achieve a just or fair result. For example, where a transfer of property has taken place, the CSA will assume that the recipient was already entitled to half of it and will therefore effectively ignore half the value of the transfer. When the application for child support is made, no account will be taken of any increase in value of the assets which have been transferred. The inevitable result is that the child support payments are likely to be assessed at an unreasonable level and it is only to be expected that the husband will use every ounce of imagination to avoid being liable to pay them.

Agreements reached by consent between the parties sound satisfactory but if either party changes their mind and wants more money or wants to pay less, they can also approach the CSA to take over their case. One way round this is to reach an agreement which is in line with what the CSA would award had they care of the case – but even then fashions change and it might get out of date. Whether it is a good idea for a government department to have a regulatory responsibility in respect of every case of child maintenance is a matter on which opinions differ. One might have thought it a matter too important to be left to the parties to decide themselves – they do not have equal bargaining power. It might also be said that this is too important a matter to be left to a government department – it ought to have the protection of the courts. The reality is of course that it takes months and months for any application to be dealt with by the CSA and it can only get worse.

How to avoid excessive assessments

The calculation of the child support is supposed to be easy but in fact it is fiendishly difficult. It has numerous features and therefore is perfect material for a dispute – in fact a considerable number of disputes. The calculation involves a number of elements which I do not propose even to enumerate. They seem to work on the basis that if you add a few arbitrary figures up, take away some others, the result is somehow fair and reasonable.

There are some serious difficulties with the regulations and calculations under the Child Support Act 1991 which make a nonsense of the whole idea. The drafting is poor, betraying a lack of understanding of Revenue law and the nature of financial provision. This creates uncertainty and confusion as well as substantial opportunities to avoid its effects, particularly in the calculation of income.

The arbitrary nature of the deductions allowed from the income means that the awards can become absurd. One or two examples will demonstrate the position. If the husband is in business they would start by looking at his business receipts which would include any amount he received from selling a capital asset. That counts as earnings for child support purposes but the cost of replacing the asset is not a deduction. (It is understood that the CSA currently consider that the proceeds of sale of a capital asset do not count as earnings for this purpose. While that is welcome, it is extremely difficult to see how their view can be supported by the Regulations and there must be a strong possibility that they will change their mind again in due course.) So if an old van is going to be replaced the husband should beware because this could have a serious effect on his child support liability. He may be making a loss and have no money which is why he sold his van to pay his creditors; that is too bad. It could be treated as income. This just encourages him to rearrange matters so that he is not disadvantaged. He would for example seek to trade in his old van at a nominal price and to pay less for the new one, or it might just encourage him to keep the old van, despite the business needs, thereby adversely affecting the earnings out of which the child support can be paid.

Alternatively he may decide to lease a van instead; the leasing payments would be fully deductible in his business accounts and would reduce his child support payments. At least they would, if it were not for the fact that the CSA regard leasing as equivalent to purchasing and will not allow all the leasing payments as a deduction, unless the asset was merely a replacement for a similar asset. Another alternative would be for him to borrow to buy a new van or other equipment because repayments on a loan to replace a capital asset are deductible in full – both interest and capital repayments. These may not be good business decisions but he may be forced to take them to avoid serious difficulties with the CSA.

Another area of injustice is in the treatment of losses – or rather the lack of recognition that losses exist. A loss sustained in one year cannot be deducted from the profits of the following year and similarly a loss made in one trade cannot be deducted from the profits of another. This seems completely to overlook the fact that losses have to be funded. Somebody has to find the money – losses cannot just be ignored. If a husband with two businesses makes a profit of £10,000 in one and a loss of £9,000 in the other, it is absurd to suggest that he has £10,000 with which to provide for himself and his children. The fact is that he has only £1,000 and if he has to pay £1,500 in child support payments he will either starve or go deeper and deeper into debt. In fact he would probably do a bit of both. Again, with such silly rules who can blame any husband who seeks to circumvent this result by every legal means at his disposal?

Another possibility worth serious consideration is to incorporate a self-employed business. He could do that quite simply by transferring the business to a limited company in which he holds all the shares. There are special income tax and capital gains tax reliefs to enable him to do this without any unnecessary tax charge – and indeed some tax advantage can be derived by making this transfer. As a director of the company he would have a salary and it will be his salary and not the earnings of the business which will determine his child support payments. This is a back-door method of getting a deduction for all the expenses which the CSA would disallow from his earnings because his salary would obviously be determined after deducting all those expenses. Indeed, his salary might be quite low – and so would his child support payments.

Further and perhaps most importantly, incorporation of the business will turn the husband into an 'employed earner' instead of a 'self-employed earner'. The regulations which define earnings of an employed earner specifically exclude 'any payment in kind' and it will be obvious by now to most readers that one way round the problem is to have all one's earnings by way of benefits in kind. The company could arrange for the groceries to be delivered, pay for all travelling and motor expenses, even provide accommodation which would include the provision of all main services and so on, leaving the individual with very little need for actual salary; all his expenses would have been met by the company. Care needs to be taken here to ensure that the benefits provided are genuine benefits and not the meeting of a pecuniary liability of the employee because that would be earnings for tax, National Insurance and therefore presumably Child Support Act purposes.

The distinction between a benefit in kind and the meeting of a pecuniary liability is really a matter of contract. If I go into a shop and buy a raincoat, I have incurred the obligation to pay for the raincoat, and if my employer reimburses me that does not affect the position. If I leave the shop with the bill made out to me and I take it to my employer who pays it, he is still discharging my liability. The discharging of an employee's liability is not a benefit in kind – it is earnings. If however the employer writes to the shop and orders a raincoat of a specific description which is to be collected by one of its employees, the employee is not personally liable to pay for the raincoat if the company fails to pay. By collecting the raincoat the employee is merely on an errand. Having collected it, the employer gives the raincoat to the employee that is a payment in kind and is not earnings. It will still be chargeable to income tax but not to National Insurance contributions, nor will it be regarded as income under the Child Support Act.

This gives a substantial opportunity to keep the income of the absent parent to the absolute minimum, but if more is needed, we can look at another exclusion from the determination of income which is one half of the amount paid by the parent to an occupational or personal pension scheme. So the absent parent, having incorporated his business and become an employee being remunerated almost entirely by benefits in kind, can now pay a pension contribution to mop up any balance of income on which the Child Support Officers may want to start doing some calculation. It is no bad thing to make pension contributions but with the CSA implications to consider it is obviously essential not to have a company pension scheme; contributions by the company to the scheme would not be contributions 'by the parent' and no part would be deductible. This has to be a personal scheme for which personal contributions need to be made.

There are special provisions to avoid manipulation of these rules:

a) Where a person has intentionally deprived himself of:
   i) any income or capital which would otherwise be a source of income;
   or

ii) any income or capital which it would be reasonable to expect would
    be secured by him;

with a view to reducing the amount of his assessable income, or

b) Where a person has performed a service either:

i) without receiving any remuneration in respect of it, or

ii) for remuneration which is less than that normally paid for the
    service

and the principal reason of the person undertaking the service without
adequate remuneration is to reduce his income for the purposes of child
support,

his income will be estimated by the Child Support Officer.

If we look at these provisions in the context of somebody
arranging his earnings so that he has only a modest salary, wholly
covered by half his pension contributions and substantial benefits,
we find that these provisions do not apply.

The husband will not have deprived himself of any income or
capital at all; he will have received proper remuneration and the
fact that it is configured in a manner which the Child Support Act
regulations specially recognize as not being earnings has not
deprived him of any income or capital. The total remuneration
package of the employee would be the salary and benefits which
could be very substantial, easily enough to represent adequate
remuneration for work undertaken so there will be no question of
him performing a service without payment.

There is a special statutory deduction of half the pension
payments which suits CSA purposes and it would be absurd to
suggest that where this deduction applies it should be disregarded because it reduces the amount of the income for CSA
purposes. The same applies with the remuneration which is
obtained largely by benefits in kind. Another alternative will be that
the husband has a portfolio of investments; that will be a source of
income and it would not be difficult to reduce the income without
depriving the husband of the source – by switching to capital
growth investments, for example, which give rise to practically no
income. The income would be reduced but the source would be
retained.

These anti-avoidance provisions are therefore likely to be effective only where the attempts to reduce the income are done in an obvious and unsophisticated manner.

Other methods have been suggested as ways round the worst excesses of the CSA. One would be to seek an order for shared residence of the child so that there would be no absent parent within the meaning of the Child Support Act 1991. Another would be to seek a child periodical payments order against the parent with care, to reimburse the expenditure incurred on contact visits; this would simply send the money round in a circle but it would alleviate the outgoings of the absent parent. Yet another would be for any deferred charge created in favour of the husband on a transfer of the matrimonial home to be increased by amounts equal to those received from the CSA.

The 1991 Act prevents any agreement being made to stop the wife applying for child support payments from the agency. However, the wording of the prohibition is only to prevent applications to the CSA; there is nothing to prevent the parties from agreeing to exclude the provisions of the 1991 Act which relate to the enforcement or collection of such maintenance. So the wife may not be prevented from applying but there will be little point in her doing so if the order cannot be enforced.

With such a capricious system the absent parent will no doubt feel fully justified in taking advantage of every element of the rules to prevent his payments being assessed wrongly. This may leave him in a better position to reach an agreement with the wife over the maintenance payments to the children without the fear of the CSA coming along and ordering him to pay insupportable amounts.

Children with means

What if the children have means of their own? This may happen by inheritance – a grandparent or godfather may leave the child a substantial sum to be used for educational purposes or generally for the child's benefit until they reach the age of eighteen or possibly twenty-five. If the sum is large it will almost certainly eliminate the obligations of the father from child support payments because the child's needs (as assessed by the CSA) will be able to be met from these funds. The important question then arises whether the wife having parental responsibility for the child would be able to get her hands on the child's money. Although in most cases she will be able to do so, the position is not at all straightforward.

The child's money will inevitably be held in trust. This may be a formal trust contained in a legal document or possibly established by a will or it may be a trust imposed by law for the protection of minors. If the trust is established by deed or by will one looks at the document to see the terms on which the money will be held and the powers of the trustees. If there is no specific document, the money just being given to the child absolutely, then the Trustee Act 1925 regulates how the money is to be dealt with. In fact, the Trustee Act will probably apply anyway because even where there is a formal document, the Trustee Act will apply unless its provisions are deliberately excluded. The overriding principle is that the money belongs to the child and it can only be used for the child's benefit.

Let us consider a simple example. Adam and Eve had a daughter Evette. When she was twelve her grandfather left her a legacy of £25,000 in his will. No trust was mentioned, the legacy being an absolute gift of cash. Although the money belongs to Evette absolutely, she cannot get her hands on it because she is under the age of eighteen and cannot give a valid receipt for the money. It will therefore be held by trustees (possibly the executors of the grandfather's estate, or possibly somebody else) who would be responsible for the money until she is eighteen. The Trustee Act therefore provides that the money will be held for Evette's benefit and will be accumulated, that is to say invested to earn interest which will be added to the capital, until she reaches the age of eighteen. On her eighteenth birthday she will receive all the money absolutely.

But what happens in the meantime? It would be cruel for Evette to have all this money accumulating for her while her mother cannot even afford to send her to school or buy her school uniform, let alone anything else. Fortunately this is not a problem. The law allows the trustees to use the money for the child's maintenance, education and benefit during her minority and these words have a comparatively wide meaning, encompassing food, clothing and holidays, as well as educational expenditure such as books (and these days no doubt such educational aids as a CD-rom drive) and school trips. The parents could apply to the trustees for money to meet various expenses for Evette's maintenance, education and benefit and the trustees would no doubt oblige – providing they are satisfied that it is really for her benefit. In this way it would be possible to use the fund to provide the costs of maintaining the child throughout her minority and this would be an entirely proper use of the money. However, one should not get carried away because the trustees would be alert to any monkey business. Evette's educational cruise around the Caribbean followed by three weeks' skiing in Colorado, accompanied of course by her parents who would need to be there to look after her, might be motivated by considerations other than Evette's best interests. However, it is really a matter for the trustees to decide bona fide whether any particular expenditure will be for her maintenance, education and benefit.

But what if Evette is a compulsive gambler, a drug addict or just foolish when it comes to money? Her grandfather's legacy will probably not last until she is twenty-two even if she does. What can be done to deprive her of her inheritance? This is a matter upon which legal advice must be taken because the consequences of getting it wrong could be very serious. You cannot simply take somebody's money away just because you think it is a good idea, and if you try to do so improperly you could end up being sued. The lawyers would no doubt consider whether the trustees could exercise their powers, either those given by the document itself or under the Trustee Act, to advance capital to her on slightly different terms so that she did not become absolutely entitled to it at the age of eighteen but so that the entitlement to capital is deferred until age twenty-five or thirty (age twenty-five is usually preferred for inheritance tax reasons). While this sounds like action to deprive Evette of her money, it could be in her best interests because it would protect the fund for her long-term benefit. Unfortunately, the power under the Trustee Act can only be used in respect of one half of the money; the other half cannot be rearranged in this way. To deal with the other half you would need to apply to the court for their permission. However, it may be that the other half of the fund would be expended during Evette's minority on her maintenance, education and benefit leaving only the other half available to be rearranged in new trusts.

Tax implications

The tax implications of the child's own funds are important because there is a substantial advantage available here. Where a minor and unmarried child receives income in their own right from money or assets provided by their parent, any income arising from that asset is taxed on the father as part of his income at his rates of tax. The income is not treated as the income of the child and therefore the personal allowances and lower rate of tax cannot be used. If however the income comes from assets not derived from the parent, for example grandparents' or godfather's gift, as in the above example (or even a step-parent) the rule for aggregating the income of the child with that of the father does not apply and the income would be regarded for tax purposes as the income of the child. As the child has a personal allowance of currently £3,525 it means that income of that amount can arise without any tax arising. It would therefore make a lot of sense to invest the money to generate as much income as possible because it would effectively be tax free.

One important point to watch here is that this tax result will only apply automatically where the assets and therefore the income belong to the child absolutely. Where the assets are held in trust, perhaps an accumulation and maintenance trust where the child becomes entitled to the income at age eighteen and the capital at age twenty-five and is accumulated in the meantime, subject to a power to pay out the income for the maintenance, education and benefit of the child, a different set of rules apply. This sounds the same but in this case the income does not belong absolutely to the beneficiary – it belongs to the trustees who merely have power to pay the money out for this purpose. The income is therefore taxable in the trustees' hands and in this type of trust the rate of tax which applies is 35 per cent. That sounds like a problem but it need not cause any difficulty because the trustees can pay out the income to the child and the child will then be able to reclaim the tax from the Inland Revenue.

5. The Family Home

The family home is likely to be the most important of the assets to be dealt with in the divorce. Not only will it probably be the most valuable asset, it may also be the home of the parties – both of whom will no doubt wish to stay there. It could also represent the family's main source of debt requiring the continuity of some serious outgoings for many years. Accordingly there are problems of ownership, division of the value, responsibility for the debt and the rights of occupation; in almost every case the interests and wishes of the parties will be in conflict. There are no easy solutions here.

Even if this does not represent an insuperable load of problems, there are also the tax implications to consider. The last thing you want when rearranging the property on a divorce is for the taxman to take a hefty bite out of already inadequate resources. There is tax relief for the mortgage interest which obviously needs to be preserved if possible, and almost whatever you do there will be a capital gains tax implication when the property is ultimately sold. And watch out if one of the partners dies because inheritance tax will be lurking in the wings; if you are not careful 40 per cent of the value of the house could go straight to the taxman.

The financial difficulties can be dealt with satisfactorily – but not by accident. You (or your lawyer and accountant) will need to give some very careful thought to all the technicalities. To give you some encouragement and just in case your advisers need a reminder of some of the points to consider, this chapter is intended to give you sufficient information to point them in the right direction.

Mortgage interest relief

The tax relief for mortgage interest is not worth a great deal these days. All you are allowed is tax relief on the interest on a mortgage of up to £30,000 and since 6 April 1995 the relief is limited to a rate of tax of only 15 per cent. This means that at the very most the tax relief for mortgage interest will be worth less than £400 per annum in terms of tax saving. When times are hard, as they often are following a divorce, every little helps, but £400 a year is not really very significant in the context of the financial implications of a divorce generally and you should not let it interfere with other more important aspects. However, obviously you should take it if you can get it.

Where the husband owns the property and after the divorce he retains the ownership and continues to meet the mortgage repayments, he will be entitled to relief for the mortgage interest even if he does not live there. If the wife pays the mortgage and has an interest in the property, she can claim the relief instead. However, if she has no interest in the property but still pays the mortgage, she is not strictly entitled to any relief although the Inland Revenue will by concession allow her the relief – but only for the matrimonial home and not for any replacement property. This concession really only applies during the period of separation and not after the divorce although the Inland Revenue will often continue to allow the relief, providing she has an interest in the property. However this cannot be guaranteed.

It may be that the husband retains the ownership of the property and pays the mortgage interest while it is occupied by the wife. He is entitled to tax relief for the mortgage interest but he cannot then claim tax relief for interest on any other mortgage – for example for the property where he lives. That is irritatingly inconvenient so in these circumstances it would be better for him to make payments to the wife so that she can pay the mortgage on the house she occupies; he can then receive relief for the interest on the mortgage for the house he occupies. In this way effectively two sets of mortgage interest relief can be obtained.

Unfortunately the above does not cover all possible situations. What if the property is owned by the wife but the husband has always paid the mortgage – and continues to do so after the divorce when he has moved out? He will not be entitled to any relief. He would be paying the mortgage on a house which he does not own and which he does not occupy. Expecting tax relief in those circumstances is perhaps a little optimistic. In such a case it would be much better for him to make payments (or increase the payments) to the wife by way of maintenance to enable her to meet the mortgage commitment. She would then be entitled to the relief.

These rules interact unfavourably with those relating to bridging finance on the acquisition of a new property. The husband may leave the matrimonial home and borrow money to acquire a property which will be his own main residence. He may feel that he should get relief on the old loan and the new loan for a period of one year but unfortunately these rules only apply where there is an intention to sell the existing house. That will probably not be the case here and this twelve-month period of double relief would therefore not apply.

Problems of ownership

The first point to consider is who actually owns the home. This is often a source of anxiety because if the husband owns the house, the wife may fear that she will lose her home if the marriage breaks down. That is a possibility, but not very likely. On the divorce, the court is most unlikely to cast the wife and children into the street – in fact they will almost certainly do exactly the reverse; they would go to great lengths to ensure that the wife and children have a roof over their heads even if this is to the substantial disadvantage of the husband.

However it is no bad thing for the wife to have an interest in the property and preferably she should try to ensure that the house is in their joint names. This can have significant advantages in the event of a dispute and in a number of other circumstance. For example:

a) In the case of a short marriage the wife could not expect to obtain a property adjustment order of half the house; even a one-third interest may be optimistic so having an existing half-interest in the house would provide a substantial degree of protection for her.

b) Where the wife is legally aided a property adjustment order in her favour whereby she obtains a half-interest in the house may be subject to a legal aid charge. This would not arise if she could show that she was already entitled to a half-interest in the property.

c) If the husband were to go bankrupt the whole of the house may be lost and the wife and children could well end up homeless. If the wife could show that she owns half the property, that half would not go to the husband's trustee in bankruptcy and she would be protected to that extent; furthermore she would be in a better position to negotiate the acquisition of the other half-interest from the trustee in bankruptcy.

d) On the death of the husband it could be important for inheritance tax purposes to identify the precise interest in the property because that will determine the estate upon which the husband is taxed. This would also be particularly important if the husband were to die intestate. If the parties are not married, the position could be substantially worse.

e) Although it would be possible for the husband to raise a loan on the security of the house, this is unlikely to be possible without the consent of the wife. He could only offer his half-interest in the house as security which is most unlikely to be satisfactory as security to any lender.

The fact that the property may be in the husband's name does not mean that he really owns it. It is a good start but all it means is that he is the 'legal owner'. What matters is who is the 'beneficial owner' and in what proportions. It could be that a husband and wife each provided half of the purchase price of the property but it was conveyed into the sole name of the husband. Unless there was some clear evidence to show that the wife intended to give her half of the property to her husband or to give him half of the purchase price, it will be treated as belonging to them equally irrespective of the name on the documents of title. The person with the legal title will hold the property as trustee for them both.

Surprisingly, however, this will not be the same the other way round. If the husband and wife each provided half the purchase price and the property is put into the name of the wife, she will not hold it as trustee for both of them. It will belong to her completely

– unless there is something positive to show that it should belong to them equally. This is because there is a legal presumption known as the presumption of advancement to the effect that any transfer of assets from the husband to the wife is presumed to be an absolute and outright gift. The presumption can be rebutted of course but it applies unless and until it is rebutted.

Now it is all very well for the wife to be the beneficial owner of half the property but how does she prove this to a third party? The husband could have borrowed against the property and the title deeds (in his name) may be held by the bank. When the husband defaults on the loan and the bank seeks to sell the property what is she to do? She may be able to prevent a sale by proving her interest in the property but she will have to prove it and that may take a good deal of time and money; furthermore, she will be caused a great deal of acute anxiety. You can have as many lawyers as you like saying that everything is all right and that you can stay in the house, but when the bank demands a sale you may begin to wonder. After all banks have lawyers too – if it was so clear why have the bank's lawyers not told the bank that they are wasting their time?

This is where Section 17 of the Married Women's Property Act 1882 comes in. Section 17 lays down the means by which the property rights of spouses can be determined. Either of them can apply to the court for a declaration of the title to the property. It might be obvious to say so but rights under the Married Women's Property Act apply only to married women and not to cohabitants. This is not a procedure which is particularly widely used because the point usually arises where there is a matrimonial breakdown and at that time the court's powers under the Matrimonial Causes Act 1973 are much more extensive; it is better for the court to deal with the property together with everything else surrounding the divorce at the same time. However, a divorce may not be imminent. The relationship may just have been deteriorating (or may be on the rocks) and the wife might feel threatened and vulnerable. A declaration under Section 17 would therefore enable her interest in the property to be determined and it could then not be taken from her except by the court; it would be protected in the event of her husband's bankruptcy and furthermore she would be free from threats (justified or not) about what might happen to the house on a divorce.

This could also assist the tax position. If the wife can establish, by securing a declaration by the court, that she owns (say) half the property, a transfer of the legal interest to her would not be a disposal or transfer for capital gains tax or inheritance tax. It would simply be the transfer to her of her own property. As we shall see, it is not always easy for assets to be transferred free of taxes from one spouse to another in a divorce and a capital gains tax charge is a genuine possibility, as some people have found to their cost. A declaration that she already owns that part of the property would obviously eliminate a possible tax charge.

Section 17 is not confined to houses, it applies to all sorts of property including investments, furniture, vehicles, money in bank accounts and jewellery and can even apply where the particular item of property has been sold. In that event the idea of the application would be to obtain an entitlement to a share of the sale proceeds. However, it must be remembered that the court merely declares ownership (although it can order a sale); it does not do anything else such as vary rights or order a transfer from one party to the other. You have to do that yourself on the back of the declaration.

If the property is in the husband's name how does the wife claim to have a partial interest in it in the first place? Unless she can show that she is entitled to part of the property, the court is only going to declare on a Section 17 application that the property belongs to the husband. A number of principles arise for the provision of an interest by the wife which can be summarized as under:

a) When the property was purchased there may have been a common intention that the property be owned jointly, despite the fact that it was conveyed into the name of the husband alone. This common intention may be evidenced by an actual agreement or it may be that she made a direct financial contribution to the purchase such as the payment of the deposit or perhaps regular contributions to the mortgage repayments.

The wife may not have made a direct contribution to the purchase but may have made a substantial indirect financial contribution such as guaranteeing the mortgage or working without pay in the husband's business to enhance the money available to him to pay the mortgage. The common intention may arise by the legal owner conducting himself in a way so as to make the other believe that she was acquiring a beneficial interest in the property. In that case the husband will be prevented from denying her interest.

b) During the period of ownership, the wife may make a substantial contribution in money or money's worth to improving the property. This includes not only money but manual work on the house and Section 37 of the Matrimonial Property and Proceedings Act 1970 gives the spouse a share in the property equal to the value of the contribution. However, this is of no application to cohabitants because the Act applies only to spouses. It may be that a cohabitant would often acquire an interest in the property for similar reasons but this could not be under the MPPA 1970.

The above has dealt with the situation where the property is in the husband's name and the wife has acquired an interest in the property by contribution or conduct. In the converse case where the husband has placed the property in the wife's name he will not be able to make the same claim to an interest in the property even though he may have provided the whole of the purchase consideration, or done all those things which would provide the wife with an interest in the property. This is because of the presumption of advancement which applies in respect of transfers of assets from a husband to a wife. This means that the transfer is presumed to be an outright and unconditional gift to the wife unless the husband can show that no gift was intended.

Quite apart from establishing that she owns a part of the property, a declaration concerning that ownership can have another perhaps unexpected advantage. Let us assume that the divorce proceedings are dragging along unsatisfactorily and it is difficult to make any progress. If the wife can establish that she owns part of the property she can (irrespective of the divorce proceedings) seek an order from the court for the property to be sold. The property would be owned jointly by herself and her husband and the general rule of jointly owned land is that either joint owner can insist on it being sold, even against the wishes of the other. There may be reasons why the court may refuse an order for sale – if, for example, the wife is in occupation and needs to continue to live there with the children – but it still represents a very powerful weapon which can be difficult to defend. This might have the effect of speeding up the divorce proceedings but obviously it cannot be done unless the wife can show that she is a joint owner.

It may be, however, that the husband owns the property alone and there are no grounds for claiming that the wife is entitled to any part of its ownership. She may receive some financial provision based on the value of the property but that is not the same thing as having a proprietary interest in the house itself. She may still have a right of occupation during the existence of the marriage (that right would cease on the divorce but may be replaced by the court order in the divorce proceedings) and it is wise for her to protect these rights in case of interference by third parties. This can be done by registering her occupation rights so that anybody buying the property or lending money on it would be made aware of her rights and could not ignore them.

The registration of her occupation rights depends upon whether the land is registered or unregistered. For registered land it involves simply sending in a form to the local land registry; for unregistered land it is necessary to register a Class F land charge at the land charges registry. The effect of these registrations is that any purchaser will buy the land subject to the occupational rights of the spouse which in practical terms means that the land cannot be sold without her knowledge and consent. Who would buy a property where the estranged wife of the vendor is still living in the property and is entitled to stay there?

The occupation rights cease on the termination of the marriage but at that time the court has the opportunity to make an order for the appropriate protection of the occupier to replace those rights.

Joint ownership

Where the house is in joint names, it is necessary to consider very carefully the nature of the joint ownership. This is extremely important and must be understood if various disasters are to be avoided. The family home in the joint names of the spouses will be held either as joint tenants or as tenants in common. The distinction is crucial. Where a property is held as joint tenants this means that on the death of one, the survivor automatically inherits the property irrespective of the terms of the deceased's will. Where the property is held as tenants in common, this will not occur; there is no right of survivorship between tenants in common and the deceased's interest in the property will pass according to the terms of his will or under the rules relating to intestacy. Accordingly, if the spouses require freedom to dispose of their share in the property as they wish, they must arrange for it to be held as tenants in common.

It may not be easy to discover how the property is held. It may have been conveyed into joint names and the conveyance may say that they hold the property as joint tenants or there may be some other evidence that this was their intention at the time of acquisition. However, although that may have been the position at the time, the joint tenancy may have been 'severed' by notice in writing by one of the joint owners or by conduct which is inconsistent with existence of a joint tenancy – such as seeking to sell the property or charging the interest to a bank – or by going bankrupt. When a joint tenancy is severed, the property becomes held as tenants in common. So it is necessary to consider not only what happened on acquisition of the property but what has happened during the period of ownership to see whether a joint tenancy continues. On the other hand, if the original documents show that the property is held as tenants in common this will continue to be the position; a tenancy in common cannot be severed.

As an example of the problems that can arise, consider the following:

Adam and Eve have both been married before and have children from their previous marriages. They decide to live separate lives but neither wants a divorce. Adam stays in the matrimonial home which is in their joint names and Eve moves into another property. On Adam's death it is expected that his half of the property will pass to his children from his first marriage and that Eve's half of the property will pass to her children. However, this will only happen if they hold the property as tenants in common. The position would be completely different if they hold the property as joint tenants. On Adam's death Eve would become entitled to his share in the property absolutely and it would pass to her by operation of law irrespective of the terms of his will. Adam's children would get no part of this property which would all devolve for the benefit of Eve's family.

Sometimes, during a period when the parties are in a harmonious relationship, the wife will be asked to agree to allow her interest in the house to be used as security for borrowings by the husband. Invariably she will be reluctant to put their house at risk but may be persuaded to do so. When the loan is called in and the bank or other debtor requires the house to be sold to repay the loan, the wife will be in serious difficulty. It may be said that she is the author of her own misfortune because she did not have to agree to the security but that is not really a fair criticism; she may have been very reluctant to do so and have been subject to very heavy emotional pressure to agree; to have refused may have cost her the marriage.

The fact that the marriage fails later does not mean that she should not have tried to preserve it by going along with her husband's wishes at the time. Anyway, what is to be done? She is obviously not in a good position and a full solution to the problem is way beyond the scope of this book; however, a few comments might be helpful.

She could claim that she entered into the transaction securing the house on the basis of undue influence. This means that somebody used a special power or position of trust and confidence to induce her to do something against her better judgement. Certain relationships create a presumption of trust and confidence – such as solicitor and client, doctor and client – in which case the transaction can be set aside unless the adviser can show that he did not abuse his position of trust and confidence or exercise undue influence in connection with the particular transaction. Unfortunately the relationship of husband and wife does not automatically give rise to a presumption of undue influence and the wife would have to show that she did in fact rely on the husband in respect of financial matters so that he would be in the necessary position of trust and confidence. If the bank knew of the circumstances that the wife had not been separately advised, it could be that the bank itself would be regarded as having exercised undue influence by reason of the fact that the wife would have trust and confidence in the bank who did not ensure that she was properly advised. If she can argue this point successfully, the ghastly consequences of her agreeing to put up her interest in the house as security for her husband's mortgage could be set aside. This possibility should not be disregarded although it must be borne in mind that the banks, alive to the possibility that they may not be able to enforce the security if they get caught up in this argument, will no doubt take the precaution of explaining the whole position to the wife, advising her to obtain independent legal advice and making sure that they are not party to, or even aware of, any representations (or misrepresentations) which might have been made by the husband so that they cannot be faulted on this ground.

Another precaution that the wife can reasonably take when asked to guarantee loans taken out by her husband is to insist that the guarantee is limited to the present amount outstanding. This may sound obvious but lenders do tend to draft guarantees so that they cover the existing indebtedness and any other indebtedness which may arise in the future. The wife can hardly be criticized for objecting to sign a blank cheque. She ought to be entitled to know what she is guaranteeing. If they want a larger guarantee later because her husband's debt has increased, it is quite reasonable for her to insist that they ask her first.

Types of order

This book is not intended to provide a definitive view on the order which will be made by the court (or agreed by the parties) in respect of the family home. It is intended to explain what the various options are, how they will affect the parties' financial position and, very importantly, the tax implications. A number of different types of order may be made.

Sale

This is the simplest and cleanest of the alternatives. The house is sold and the proceeds divided between the parties either in accordance with their ownership, after having their respective ownership rights considered, or in some other way that the court may direct. For example the court may decide that the wife has a one-third interest in the property and may order that the proceeds of sale accruing to the husband from his two-thirds will enable him to make a lump sum payment to the wife as part of the financial provision on the divorce.

However, in many cases a sale will be impossible because one of the parties (and of course the children) needs a roof over their heads. It is all very well for the husband to say that he wants his money and needs it to buy somewhere to live, but the court does not necessarily see things in quite the same way. The need to house the children will take priority over the husband's requirements. If there are no children and it will not interfere with housing both the parties, an order would probably be made that the house be sold to facilitate a clean break enabling each spouse to go their own separate ways without any continuing financial relationship. However, quite often that cannot be done so easily and the more usual position is that the wife and children will continue to live in the house.

This obviously gives rise to a number of problems because the husband may have a good deal of money (which he will need) tied up in the house; he may also have a substantial mortgage which he needs to continue to pay and which thereby restricts his opportunity to buy another house. It may be unfair to ask him to give the whole of the house to the wife – so what can be done? The answer is usually some kind of order which protects the husband's property rights in the long term but at the same time protects the wife's rights of occupation. The first type of order to mention is a Mesher order.

Mesher order

The essence of a Mesher order is that the house is retained during the minority of the children. During this period the wife resides in the house rent free but on payment of the relevant outgoings and when the children reach their majority the house is sold and the proceeds divided between the parties. The order derives from the case of Mesher v. Mesher decided in 1973 and its simplicity was perhaps based on the fact that in this case the husband was satisfactorily housed elsewhere and the wife was intending to marry somebody else.

Unfortunately these good intentions can have the effect of trapping all the parties into an unsatisfactory position. This is made worse by the fact that there is no statutory power to vary a Mesher order once it has been made. A number of variations have emerged to cope with the problems arising from a Mesher order. For example it is unsatisfactory that on the eighteenth birthday of the youngest child the house should be sold and the wife rendered homeless. The family will not simply disappear at that moment. The house will still be their home and to break it up at such a time is not easily defensible. The wife will be in no better position to rehouse herself at this time because she has spent the whole of the period of occupation caring for the children. The problem really ceases to be a question of putting a roof over the head of the children but of providing a continuing roof for the spouse.

Unfortunately things are not quite so simple. Funds have to be available to meet the requirements of the parties and a number of variations have developed. One not very helpful alternative is that the house is retained until the children reach the age of eighteen or cease full-time education, and this could be combined with a provision that the house is sold if the wife remarries or if she dies or if she moves voluntarily.

Martin order

The Martin order sprang from the potential defect in the Mesher order which is that it was predominantly for the benefit of the children. In Martin it was said that there was no magic in the fact that there were children to be considered. That just meant that their interests took priority. If it was a rule that when the children reach the age of eighteen the house is to be sold then a great deal of hardship can build up. The principle established in this case is that the primary concern is for both parties to have, if possible, a roof over their heads. A Martin order therefore causes the house to be held in trust for the wife during her lifetime, remarriage or until she leaves the property voluntarily, and thereafter it would be sold and the proceeds divided between the parties as appropriate. While this solves the occupation problem for the wife and enables the husband to retain his investment in the property, this is not much use to the husband as his investment is effectively sterilized. He will be stuck with the mortgage taken out to buy the property and have no opportunity to realize his investment and get rid of the millstone of debt. The resolution of the problem will obviously depend upon the figures and the resources of the husband but in the end it will be a problem for the court to weigh up the facts and apportion the hardship between the husband and wife.

A Martin order does have the advantage of a clean break combined with some comfort for the husband that if his wife remarries he will get his money and it will not unfairly benefit her new husband.

Transfer to spouse

One way of avoiding these difficulties if funds permit is for the court to order that the house be transferred to the wife outright. If she is in a position to obtain and service a mortgage then a purchase by the wife of the husband's share of the property has a great deal to commend it. It would extinguish the husband's rights to the house, creating the desirable clean break, and free the husband from debt, giving him a chance to house himself. It would also provide much greater freedom of action for the wife to do as she pleases with her life without the constant threat that she may lose the right to occupy the house.

Occupation rent

Any of the above orders, whereby the wife remains in occupation and the rights in the property are maintained but deferred, necessarily involve hardship to the husband for loss of his capital. One way to restore this is for the wife to pay a rent for her occupation – although this will very rarely be ordered during the minority of the children. This is a way of compensating the husband for being deprived of his proceeds of the sale of the house and it may be pitched at a level which both sides can afford. While this has some attraction it can be a disaster for tax purposes because the rent would be treated as taxable income in the hands of the husband without any tax deduction by the wife. It therefore creates a tax liability out of thin air and is not to be recommended. There are arguments that the rent is not technically rent for tax purposes and while the possibility is attractive, there are other grounds available to the Inland Revenue to bring it into charge to income tax. However, if the parties like the idea of an occupational rent and apart from the tax implications it would suit their financial circumstances, a variation on this theme could be contrived which does not have such adverse tax consequences. For example, an order could be devised whereby the wife occupies the house rent free with the children until they reach the age of eighteen and on that occasion she would be obliged to purchase her husband's interest in the property for a specified sum payable in monthly or quarterly instalments. Those instalments might be rather similar to the rent which might otherwise have been payable but their character would be quite different and no income tax would arise.

Deferred charge

This is yet another variation containing a number of the same features. What happens here is that the home is transferred to the spouse in occupation but subject to a charge payable at some later date – when the property is sold, say. The charge could be a fixed amount or it could be a proportion of the value of the house subject to the mortgage. This does not really have any advantages over the previous ideas because it really amounts to the same thing. It also suffers from the same drawback that on sale, the proceeds may be insufficient to allow the wife to rehouse herself. The only possible advantage here is that once the property has been transferred to the wife, the mortgagee may be prepared to release the husband from his obligations under the mortgage because he no longer has any interest in the property. That may make it easier for him to obtain a mortgage of his own on an alternative home. Unfortunately, however, the tax implications are so ghastly (see below) that the idea of a deferred charge should only rarely be considered.

The tax implications

The tax implications of the various orders the court may make at their own discretion or at the request of the parties under a consent order have significantly different tax implications and it is obviously extremely important that you do not end up with an order that sounds fine but costs you a fortune in tax. The capital gains tax and inheritance tax implications surrounding the various arrangements must therefore be considered very carefully if the pitfalls are to be avoided. Professional advice will almost certainly be required here even if the parties are in (almost) total harmony because you need to ensure that the arrangements giving effect to their wishes do not inadvertently fall foul of the taxman.

Chapter 2 sets out the general scheme of capital gains tax and how the tax charge arises. In the context of a transfer of the family home some special considerations have to be looked at, particularly in relation to the exemption from capital gains tax for the main residence.

It will be remembered that transfers of assets between spouses in a divorce give rise to a serious capital gains tax problem. If we assume that a couple separate and, prior to the formal divorce proceedings, the husband transfers to the wife a property, possibly as part of her expected financial entitlement in the divorce, this will be a catastrophe in terms of tax. The husband and wife are still married – they will continue to be married until the marriage is dissolved by the decree absolute and accordingly they are necessarily connected persons. This means that the transfer of the house must be treated as if it was a sale by the husband to the wife at market value. At this point they may say, what does it matter? If we are connected persons because we are still married, it follows that the relief for transfer between husbands and wives will apply to eliminate any taxable gain. But no. The relief for transfers between husband and wife only applies if they are living together so the worst of both worlds will apply. A gain is deemed to arise and there is no escape from the charge to tax. This sounds like a disaster and it was for the parties in the case of Apsden v. Hildsley in 1981, but if you see the problem coming you can do something about it. If you think back to Section 17 of the Married Women's Property Act 1882 and the possibility of obtaining a declaration from the court about who owns the property, this problem can be sidestepped – at least partly. If the wife were to obtain a declaration from the court that she already held a 50 per cent interest in the property by reason of her own contributions, the transfer of the property to her would only be a transfer of the husband's half-share. That halves the problem – which is a good start.

Another possibility is hold-over relief. It may be remembered that hold-over relief only applies to the gift of business assets and to gifts chargeable to inheritance tax; neither would seem to apply here. However, it can perhaps be contrived. One way to do this would be to transfer the asset into a discretionary trust. That would be a chargeable transfer for inheritance tax purposes and inheritance tax would be payable if it were not for the fact that the first £154,000 of chargeable transfers are chargeable at the rate of nil. This is a funny way of saying that there will not be any tax to pay but there are technical reasons for it. The effect is that hold-over relief would apply because this would be a transfer technically chargeable to inheritance tax. The idea would be for the husband to transfer the property to trustees for the benefit of his wife claiming hold-over relief so that no gain arises on the transfer; providing she is the main beneficiary and the trustees are persons she trusts, she would not be significantly disadvantaged because she would ultimately become entitled to the capital and in the meantime she would have the benefit of the occupation. In this way the property would be effectively transferred by the husband to the wife without any tax liability arising and the objective would be achieved.

An example might make this easier to understand.

Husband and wife have a holiday home which cost £40,000 in 1985 but is now worth £150,000. They are separated and it is intended that the house (which belongs to the husband) be transferred to the wife. A straightforward transfer would be treated as a sale by the husband for £150,000 and the capital gains tax would be calculated as under:

Deemed proceeds		£150,000
Cost	£40,000	
Indexation relief (say 75%)	£28,000	£68,000
		£82,000
Less husband's annual exemption		£6,000
		£76,000
Capital gains at 40%	£30,400	

This is a lot of tax to pay when nobody is buying anything – just transferring an asset under protest to the wife. It would obviously be preferable for no tax to arise and that is where hold-over relief can come in useful.

Let us assume that instead of transferring the property to the wife, the husband transfers it to a discretionary trust in which the wife is the main beneficiary. This would be a chargeable transfer for inheritance tax purposes but a transfer of £150,000 would give rise to no tax because it is within the nil rate band. The husband could make a claim to hold over the gain of £82,000 so that the trustees would be treated as acquiring the property at a price of £68,000 – the husband's cost price as enhanced by the indexation. The wife occupies the property rent free under the terms of the trust and in due course the property could be distributed to the wife absolutely, although there would seem to be no compelling reason to do so. As we shall see later, this arrangement not only avoids the capital gains tax charge on the transfer to the wife, but also enables the private residence exemption to be obtained by the trustees.

A technical point arises here which must be considered very carefully in connection with this technique. The hold-over relief which is being sought applies only where the transfer is for no consideration or at least where the consideration is less the donor's base cost. If these arrangements were made pursuant to a court order there would be an element of bounty because the transfer would have been made in consideration of the partial or complete abandonment of the claims which the wife would have by way of alternative financial provision in the divorce. The same reasoning would apply to preclude a hold-over relief claim without a court order if the arrangements were made for this purpose. If, however, the husband were to establish the settlement and transfer the property to the trustees not as part of any settlement for the wife but merely to place his assets in a more convenient configuration for the meeting of his obligations, there will be no consideration for the transfer and hold-over relief should apply.

Main residence exemption

There is a capital gains tax exemption of enormous importance and that is the exemption for the principal private residence. The general rule is that when you sell your only or main residence the gain is exempt, and this extends not just to the house but to land which is for the occupation and enjoyment with the house up to half a hectare or as large an area as is required for the reasonable enjoyment of the property as a residence. It is perhaps unnecessary to dwell on how large an area of garden or grounds can qualify for the exemption, but if the house is substantial this is certainly an aspect which would repay considerable attention. The figures would always be sufficiently high to warrant professional advice, but before doing so you should collect together as many facts (and photographs if there are any) to show that the house was of a size and nature that a large area was required for the reasonable enjoyment of it as a residence. The fact that you did use it all as garden or grounds would obviously be persuasive evidence in your favour. If, however, the garden area was small and delineated by a fence, the remainder of the land being grazing for bulls or other animals the presence of which would mean that you could not reasonably use that area as garden or grounds, that would obviously be unhelpful. One or two crucial points in connection with this relief need to be highlighted. For example, a husband and wife are only entitled to one main residence exemption between them. The exemption is given only to the person who owns the interest in the property; it is generally not possible to obtain the exemption in respect of somebody else's house. It is not available unless it is the only or main residence of the person making the gain and if you have two homes you have to make an election as to which one you would like to be treated as your main residence – there are strict time limits for making this election. So it is no good if you do not live there. However, where a house has at any time qualified for the exemption, the last three years of ownership will be exempt whether they are occupied or not.

In the context of a matrimonial breakdown you must watch the conditions very carefully. If at any time during your period of ownership the property has been your only or main residence, you are entitled to claim the exemption – not for the whole gain but only for the time when it was your main residence, plus of course the last three years in any event. So if you bought it, let it for four years, then lived in it for another four years before selling it at a profit, half the gain would be exempt and half would be chargeable. If, however, you lived in the property for four years and then let it for four years before selling it, only one eighth of your profit would be chargeable. Three of the four years which would otherwise have been disqualified from relief will be eligible for relief because they are the three years immediately prior to the sale.

The Inland Revenue recognize the problems which can arise with the exemption where couples separate or are divorced. If they both continue to occupy the property, obviously the exemption will continue to apply, but invariably one party will move out. If we assume that the couple own the property jointly and the husband moves out but as part of the financial settlement he disposes of his interest in the property to the wife, this is potentially a disaster because he could end up with a huge capital gain. The private residence exemption can come to the rescue – but not of course for any period after he has moved out because for that period it was not his main residence. In these circumstances the Inland Revenue by Concession D6 (a concession you can rely on – it will not and cannot be denied you at the whim of the Inland Revenue providing you satisfy its conditions precisely) will regard the property as continuing to be the husband's main residence for the purpose of this exemption providing the wife continues to live in the property and the husband has not elected that another property should be treated as his main residence for this period. The concession says:

> Where a married couple separate or are divorced and one partner ceases to occupy the matrimonial home and subsequently as part of a financial settlement disposes of the home, or an interest in it, to the other partner, the home may be regarded for the purposes of [the capital gains tax private residence exemption] as continuing to be a residence of the transferring partner from the date his or her occupation ceases until the date of transfer, provided that where it has throughout this period been the other partner's only or main residence. Thus where a husband leaves the matrimonial home while still owning it, the usual capital gains tax exemption or relief for a taxpayer's only or main residence would be given on the subsequent transfer to the wife provided she has continued to live in the house and the husband has not elected that some other house should be treated for capital gains tax purposes as his main residence for this period.

The terms of this concession are very restrictive, requiring, for example, a transfer to the other spouse, and do not include a sale by either spouse to a third party. If that is what is required it will be necessary for the husband first to transfer to the wife the interest in the house and for her then to sell the property to the third party. In that way the Concession D6 would exempt the transfer to the wife, and the wife's gain would be entirely exempt because the exemption would apply to her in full; the ultimate sale proceeds would therefore be tax free.

If this transfer takes place within three years of the husband moving out this concession is unnecessary because the exemption would still be available under the strict rules; he will always be entitled to the exemption for the last three years of ownership even if he elects for another property to be his main residence. However, after the three years are up he will start to lose the exemption and the problem will get progressively worse – particularly in the case of a Mesher type of order where there may be a very long delay before a sale takes place.

This places the husband in a dilemma because he must make a choice between an exemption in respect of his interest in the house occupied by his wife, or in respect of his own home. He will of course want an exemption on both and some further planning is therefore required.

An extremely useful extension to the exemption is that which is given to trustees. In the perfectly normal situation where a husband dies and leaves his estate in trust for his widow during her lifetime and thereafter to the children, a problem would arise with the family home. If the widow were to sell the house, perhaps to move to a smaller house or to be nearer her children, any gain made on the sale of the house would not benefit from the exemption. While she would occupy the house as her main residence, it would not be the widow who would make the gain – it would be the trustees. However, the trustees would not be occupying the property and could not claim the exemption. The problem is that the owner and the occupier are different people so neither can satisfy the conditions for the exemption. To deal with this obvious unfairness there is a special provision Section 225 Taxation of Chargeable Gains Act 1992 which says that where the property has been the only or main residence of the person entitled to occupy it under the terms of the trust, the trustees would be entitled to the exemption in the normal way. (This also applies to beneficiaries of a discretionary trust who occupy the property at the discretion of the trustees and not only by reason of an express term of the trust.)

This provides an opportunity to obtain an extra exemption for a property occupied by a relative, friend or perhaps secret companion, without parting with the value of the property. By placing the property in discretionary trust with the occupier within a case of beneficiary, the trustees will gain the exemption by reason of the occupation of the beneficiary.

There is no limit to the number of trusts which can be set up –

subject to your willingness to provide residences for other people. Each trust is looked at entirely separately and providing the above conditions are satisfied, the exemption will be available.

There is also a Concession D26 operated by the Inland Revenue where two individuals are joint owners of properties which are their respective homes and they exchange their interests so that each becomes the sole owner of the house in which they live. Strictly this would give rise to a capital gains tax charge on both of them but the concession allows the exchange to take place effectively at cost so that no gains arise. This can be particularly helpful in circumstances where for example the couple own two properties jointly and after the separation the husband moves into the other property. It might also be useful if the husband stays put in the jointly owned matrimonial home and buys another house in their joint names into which the wife moves. Concession D26 will enable them to rearrange their ownership of the property without any capital gains tax charge.

With the general background it is appropriate to consider the effect of the capital gains tax rules on the types of order referred to above.

Sale or transfer to spouse

In most cases a sale will not give rise to any capital gains tax problem. Both parties would have lived in the property at some time as their main residence and the gain is therefore likely to be fully exempt. If one or other of the parties has moved out and the sale takes place within three years the capital gains tax exemption would not be affected. If, however, the husband has moved out for more than three years and he still owns a share in the property, he would want to ensure that he does not elect for any other property to be his main residence in which case he could claim the benefit of Concession D6 and be treated as continuing to reside in the property for the purposes of the exemption. As mentioned above the Concession D6 would not apply in these circumstances because it only applies to a sale to the other spouse in occupation so it would be necessary if a sale is being made to a third party to transfer the property to the wife first. The problem with this is that the husband's other house in which he may have lived for the last three years will not qualify for the exemption for that period when it is ultimately sold. There is no three-year period on acquisition to help him and by claiming Concession D6 he is just trading one exemption (on the house he occupies) for another (on the house his wife occupies). This is clearly a circumstance where the wife would be well advised to have sought an order under Section 17 of the Married Women's Property Act 1882 declaring the extent of her interest so that the capital gains tax damage is limited only to her husband's share. She may not care much about her husband's tax liability but she would prefer to avoid any liability herself. She might be prepared to help because to the extent that her husband is faced with an unnecessary tax liability, he will be left with less money to make financial provision for her.

One way of dealing with the potential problem here is for the husband to place his interest in the property into trust for the benefit of himself and his wife shortly after he moves out perhaps on a without-prejudice basis. At first sight this may seem a little odd. However, remember that what he wants to do is to retain the capital value for himself (subject to the court forcing him to give it away) and to preserve his capital gains tax exemption on the house while at the same time obtaining another exemption on his new home. This may seem like an impossible objective but a trust enables it to be achieved. If he transfers the house to a trust in which he and his wife were both beneficiaries but in which he has a life interest (that is the primary income entitlement) under the settlement no inheritance tax would arise nor would the transfer to the trustees give rise to any capital gains tax because he would at that time benefit from the main residence exemption. The trustees would have power to allow any beneficiary (that is including the wife) to occupy the property as her only or main residence. The whole point here is the special provision in Section 225 of the Taxation of Chargeable Gains Act 1992: where the property is sold the trustees would be entitled to the exemption in full if the property has been used by one of the beneficiaries as their main residence. The existence of the wife's occupation validates the exemption by the trustees and this does not affect the capital gains tax that the husband can still obtain on his own house. In this way two main residence exemptions are obtained without any disadvantages at all.

Mesher and Martin orders

It will be remembered that under these orders the husband retains his interest in the matrimonial home but the sale is postponed during the minority of the children (that would be a normal Mesher order) or for the lifetime of the wife (that would be a normal Martin order) subject in both cases to the remarriage of the wife or her voluntary departure from the property. In strictness these arrangements will usually represent a trust and the tax implications will follow the creation of that trust. This is not really a problem providing you know the tax rules which apply.

The first point to appreciate is that when an asset becomes 'settled property' this is considered a disposal for capital gains tax purposes and a capital gains tax liability may therefore arise. Let us assume a conventional Martin order where the husband retains his interest in the property until such time as the wife dies, remarries or moves out of her own accord. At least in the view of the Inland Revenue this would create a trust and the husband (and the wife too if she has an interest in the property) would be treated for capital gains tax purposes as if they had sold the property at market value to the trustees (the trustees would of course be the husband and wife themselves). It would not matter if this takes place within three years of the husband moving out because in that event any gain arising to the husband on his disposal will be exempt. Unfortunately, if this takes place more than three years after the separation, Concession D6 will not apply to assist the husband because the disposal deemed to take place on the creation of the settlement is not 'to the other spouse' which is a requirement of the concession. It should also be remembered that hold-over relief will not apply here because the asset is not within a qualifying class. However, the property will be held in trust and a beneficiary, the wife, will be occupying the property under the terms of the settlement, so any ultimate disposal by the trustee will be free of capital gains tax because of the private residence exemption – our old friend Section 225 applies. So when the property is sold the proceeds can be distributed to the husband and wife in the appropriate proportions without any unnecessary tax arising.

Deferred charge

In this type of order the house would be transferred to the wife in occupation subject to the husband's right to a share in the sale proceeds on ultimate sale. The husband's entitlement may be a fixed amount or a proportion of the sale proceeds and will be subject to a charge on the property. What has happened here is that there has been a sale of the husband's interest in the house to the wife for a deferred consideration. If this order is made within three years of the husband moving out of the property, Concession D6 would apply and no tax would arise by reason of the private residence exemption. However, what happens in due course when the property is sold and the husband receives his money? Sale proceeds receivable by the wife would be free of tax in her hands because the property continues to be her main residence. But what of the husband? If he merely receives a fixed amount, no problem would arise because that would have been the amount for which he sold the property to the wife at the date of the order. No gain would therefore arise; he would merely be having his outstanding debt paid. If however he receives a proportion of the sale proceeds he may receive a great deal more than the amount it was worth when the order was made. In that event what he will have done is to have sold his interest in the property to the wife at the date of the order for an uncertain consideration payable at some time in the future. He would no longer have any interest in the property but would have the right to receive an unquantified amount of money. This would not be a debt because a debt has to be a quantified amount; it would just be a right to receive an amount of money in the future. This would be an asset for capital gains tax, the acquisition cost of which would be the value of that right at the date of the order and the right would be disposed of when the property is ultimately sold and his proportion of the sale proceeds is paid to him in satisfaction.

A gain will almost always arise because the property will probably have gone up in value however depressed the property market. This gain is not made from the disposal of a private residence and cannot therefore be exempt; it is just the disposal of some uncertain rights to which the capital gains tax exemption cannot apply. For the same reason Concession D6 cannot apply either. An example may assist in clarifying the position.

> Adam and Eve own their home jointly and as part of the divorce proceedings Adam is ordered to transfer his interest in the property to Eve, subject to a right for Adam to receive half the proceeds in the event of sale. The property is worth £200,000 at the date of the order. The market value of Adam's half interest is therefore approximately £100,000. (In practice it is likely that it would be valued somewhat less because a partial interest in a property is invariably worth less than a direct proportion of the whole; this is because the other part owner can interfere with your full enjoyment of the property.) However, in due course Eve sells the property for £300,000 and the sale proceeds are divided equally between them. Adam therefore makes a taxable gain of £50,000 because when he transferred his interest to Eve it was deemed to be transferred to her at market value of £100,000. He acquired a right to receive one half of the proceeds of sale in due course, and that right had been acquired at a cost of £100,000, the market value of his interest at the time. So when Adam receives his £150,000, half the ultimate sale proceeds, he makes a £50,000 gain and is taxed upon it. No capital gains tax exemption applies.

This would obviously be most unsatisfactory from Adam's point of view and what is more it is entirely unnecessary. Exactly the same division of proceeds could have been achieved by an order whereby the property is held in trust for them both in equal shares but with the wife having rights of occupation for the relevant period. In that way the capital gains tax position would be almost identical to a Mesher or Martin order and no capital gains tax liabilities would occur. For this reason a deferred charge is always to be avoided in favour of an alternative which allows a capital gains tax exemption to be obtained.

Inheritance tax

No inheritance tax implications should arise in respect of any of the above transfers because even if the parties are not married at the time of the transfer and therefore ineligible for the spouse exemption, the transfers would have been made by reason of a court order. This means that it would not be regarded as a disposition intended to confer a gratuitous benefit (in other words it would not be a gift) and it would therefore be outside the scope of inheritance tax. Even if the transfer were to be made other than by way of a court order it could still be exempt from inheritance tax under another provision, being a transfer from one party to a marriage to the other for the maintenance of a former spouse on the occasion of the dissolution of the marriage. Even if neither of the above applies it is still unlikely to be a big problem because the transfer is likely to be a potentially exempt transfer and not chargeable unless the transferor dies within seven years.

6. Pension Rights

The problem explained – and some solutions

The court is bound to have regard to the loss of pension rights by reason of the divorce. You will remember that it is one of the matters to which specific attention is directed by the Matrimonial Causes Act 1973. However it provides no guidelines or powers about how pension rights should be dealt with. Where the couple remain married the wife will have some financial protection on the retirement, incapacity or death of her husband by reason of his pension provision. It may be a lump sum on death or a widow's pension, or merely the right to benefit from her husband's pension for financial support during his retirement. Even without any private pension arrangements the wife can enjoy a pension herself based on her husband's contributions. After the divorce the wife is no longer able to rely on the husband's contributions in this way and she may have been denied the opportunity to build up her own pension by her devotion to the home and children.

She will continue to be entitled to benefit from her husband's contributions up to the date of the divorce but not thereafter. If she remarries before reaching the age of sixty, she will have to rely on her new husband's contributions, or alternatively make her own contributions, perhaps voluntarily under Class 3 to maintain her state pension rights. This can give rise to a serious loss for which the wife requires proper compensation. And what if he dies after the divorce – she gets nothing unless the maintenance is secured or she has a lump sum. Nor will she receive any state benefits like a widow's pension. The husband can protect her position by taking out insurance to protect her in the event of his death; that is a very good idea but unfortunately the court has no power to order it. However, it can (and should) feature in any consent order and all the arrangements should be made before the final order while the wife has an insurable interest in her husband's life.

With private occupational pension schemes there is a further difficulty. The pension rights cannot just be cashed in and divided up and in most cases the court cannot just direct that the pension fund be held partly for the ex-wife. The pension scheme is governed by rules and although normally they will provide for a widow's pension to be payable, an ex-wife will no longer qualify as a widow; there is no concept of an ex-widow. And what if he had more than one wife? The pension could hardly be shared between a wife and the ex-wife or a number of ex-wives. Even where there is no other candidate, a divorced ex-wife may not be within the class of persons eligible to benefit under the pension fund. You could get an undertaking for the husband to nominate the wife as a beneficiary in the event of his death but unfortunately that would not necessarily bind the trustees of the pension scheme. In any event once he is dead what can you do if you find that he had revoked it? However, the existence of the pension fund may be enough to enable the court to order a lump sum to be paid to her by way of financial provision for the loss of these rights.

But do be careful. Personal pension plans will not usually provide any benefit to the wife unless the husband makes a specific election. If he has not done so, how can the wife claim that she loses anything by the divorce because she was not entitled to anything before the divorce?

The pension scheme might provide that no widow's pension is payable after separation. That is exactly the position with Army pensions. In that case the wife again would suffer no loss for which she should be compensated. She would have no entitlement to lose by reason of the divorce. It would be a wise move for the wife who is planning a separation to make some discreet enquiries about the pension scheme before she does so.

A woman who has been receiving maintenance up to the date of the death of her former husband would have a good case under the

Inheritance (Provision for Family and Dependants) Act 1975 because she would be a person who was being wholly or partially maintained by the deceased immediately before his death. A claim for part of the lump sum payable from the pension fund might therefore be possible, although this may need to be divided between her and his new wife (and possibly other dependants).

Recently the courts have developed an argument that a pension scheme established by the husband's company is a postnuptial settlement and therefore capable of variation by the court thereby providing her with a pension. The reasoning is complex and the same result would not necessarily apply in every case. No order by the court would be possible, for example, if third parties (i.e. other pension scheme members) were affected and this could be a serious obstacle where there are lots of members of the pension fund. Furthermore, had the wife not actually been an employee of the company at the time there could well be difficulties with the Inland Revenue withdrawing approval for the scheme exposing the funds to a tax charge. For the wife to succeed with the argument it is necessary to show not only that the pension scheme was a marriage settlement but also that the variation for her benefit would not prejudice other members of the pension scheme – apart from the husband of course. This could be really difficult and many people feel that this recent case of Brooks v Brooks (1995) was so unusual because the facts were extremely convenient (in fact perfect to support Mrs Brooks' argument) and are unlikely to be repeated in another case.

Where this treatment is impossible, and a lump sum cannot sensibly be ordered because the husband simply has no capital (or ability to borrow enough) to pay appropriate compensation, the only solution would seem to be to avoid any kind of clean break which would otherwise have been desirable and to seek periodical payments. At least this would preserve the wife's right to seek a variation in her maintenance when the pension arises but that would obviously cease on his death. A good alternative would be to seek a lump sum deferred until the husband has the opportunity to commute part of his pension to a lump sum. The courts are rather reluctant to order a lump sum payable at some long time in the future – it seems that ten years might be the upper limit. But it should be borne in mind that pensions are not always as secure as they look; the experience of those who suffered at the hands of Mr Maxwell should not be forgotten.

Where the husband is in the armed services there is a statutory prohibition against interfering with the service pension. This seems to prevent the court from making a deferred or contingent order for payment of a lump sum out of the prospective pension entitlement. However, it would appear that this extends only to the prospective pension benefits and not to pension monies which have already been received.

Where the loss of pension rights would be a serious problem and there is no sensible means of providing adequate compensation, the wife might be content with a decree of judicial separation. She would therefore remain his wife and ultimately would become the widow, fully entitled to the pension benefits which would ordinarily accrue to the widow. This will not always be convenient, particularly if remarriage is contemplated by either party, but this possibility could give a tactical advantage to the wife to insist on adequate insurance or alternative financial protection if the husband seeks a divorce.

Another alternative would be for the wife to make an application under Section 5 of the Matrimonial Causes Act 1973 to prevent the divorce on the grounds that the decree would cause her grave financial or other hardship. The hardship must be really serious (divorce inevitably involves some hardship) and it must arise from the decree itself. The loss of valuable pension benefits is an obvious example but the court would need to see whether these could be compensated in some other way. If the husband, for example, puts forward proposals for the provision of an annuity from an insurance company which would alleviate the hardship or at least reduce it to below a level which would be 'grave' the court may well allow the decree on this basis. This may be a back-door means for the wife to ensure that the husband provides adequate compensation for the loss of pension rights even if the court is unable to order it directly.

It will be appreciated that the problems associated with the loss of pension rights on divorce can be extremely vexed and the government are earnestly trying to find a solution. Unfortunately nothing workable has yet emerged but there is a clear willingness to solve the problem. In the meantime, the above methods of alleviating the position may be all that is available to the wife.

7. The Family Business

It is quite usual to find a husband and wife who both work in the family business. They may have started it together and built it up or perhaps pressures of one kind or another may have encouraged one spouse to give up what they were doing and join the other in developing or helping in the business. Whatever the motives, the business may have been carried on by both of them, possibly in partnership or through a limited company and it may have grown to a size where it has assumed a significant value.

Then comes the parting of the ways. This may lead (but by no means necessarily) to a withdrawal of one spouse from participation in, but not from the ownership of, the business. The departing spouse may not want to work with the other but is clearly not going to hand over the whole of their interest in the business to the other for nothing. However, a problem does arise here. Let us assume that a couple have a successful business which they operate through a company in which they each hold 50 per cent of the shares. That might be thought to be rather similar to a partnership and in many ways it would be. They are both directors, they both have an equal shareholding in the company but now they want to go their own ways. But who is going to buy out whom – and at what price? Unfortunately there is no easy answer to this and you need to be aware of the implications so that you do not start trying to win a hopeless argument or fail to construct a good argument for the best financial settlement.

The party who continues with the business would seem to have the upper hand. Let us assume that this is the husband. He can work in the business and draw a salary and the wife who withdraws from the business clearly merits no salary – she is not doing any work. So the husband still has got an income but the wife has not. She still owns half-shares in the company and her husband's continuing efforts may enhance the value of her shares – providing she can sell them at some stage.

She might want her husband to buy her shares – but why should he? He is happy with his lot so why should he fork out a large sum of money to acquire a further stake in the business? He can just let her stew – and under the circumstances he will probably want to do just that. She cannot force him to buy – still less at the price she would like, so the one who stays with the business would seem to have the advantage.

However, it need not be like that. The wife is not really at such a disadvantage as it might seem. The husband may still be running the business and drawing a salary but she would be a director and entitled to participate in the decision-making process. She may not want to do so and she certainly would be unwise to get into arguments about the business which might damage it and her investment, but she is entitled to know what is going on. She is therefore able to keep an eye on what her husband is doing and this may discourage him from doing anything in particular to her disadvantage. In fact, she can be a real pain in the neck. As a director she is entitled to be invited to all directors' meetings and entitled to be consulted on all relevant matters. She can insist on being given all this information and can cause the most almighty fuss if she is not. With only 50 per cent of the voting power the husband may find that he cannot do things that he would like to do because he does not have control of the company – that needs more than 50 per cent. He will constantly have to seek her agreement to do things and this gives her the opportunity to encourage him to buy her shares.

It may be that in the normal course of events, depending upon the terms of the Articles of Association, the directors would retire by rotation every three years and come up for re-election. To re-elect a director requires 51 per cent of the votes. Whoever retires first by rotation is therefore likely to be at a significant disadvantage; he will not be re-elected without the votes of the other. But again that is not the end of the world; if the husband comes up for re-election the wife can extract from him various undertakings including his promise, in legally binding form, that he will not frustrate her re-election when she retires the following year.

As a shareholder the wife will be entitled to notice of all meetings and entitled to vote on all ordinary and special resolutions and indeed no such resolutions can possibly be passed without her consent. All these things can make life extremely difficult for the husband who may therefore feel it more in his interests to buy his wife's shares.

One then moves to the question of how much he should pay. Inevitably the answer is that the price to be paid for these shares will have nothing to do with their intrinsic worth but how much she can screw out of him or his advisers or how little he can persuade her or her advisers to accept.

Unincorporated businesses

Not all businesses are run through limited companies. Many family companies are run by a single proprietor or perhaps a number of individuals in partnership. Where the husband and wife carry on business together a question might arise about the size of the wife's share of the business. She would be greatly comforted by the following words of Lord Denning from a case in 1969 – although it would be unwise to place too much reliance on it because times have changed a little since 1969.

> Up and down the country a woman helps her husband in the business. She serves in the shop. He does the travelling around. If the shop and business belonged to him before they married no doubt it will remain his after they marry. But she by her work afterwards should get some interest in it. Not perhaps an equal share but some share. If they acquire the shop and business after they marry – and acquire it by their joint efforts – then it is their joint property no matter that it is taken in the husband's name. In such a case when she works in the business afterwards she becomes virtually a partner in it and she is entitled prima facie to an equal share.

It was mentioned earlier in connection with the role of accountants that it will rarely be possible to arrive at an exact figure. It will
be a judgement. It will also be tempting to look at the value of the
business if it were to be sold but this will not usually be relevant; in
most cases the business will certainly not be sold. However, it will
still need to be valued and this can be approached in a number of
ways; of course it will always depend upon who is asking – is it a
buyer or a seller – but in any event it will usually be necessary to
start on the basis of the assets owned by the business. You will
know what the assets are because they would be shown in the
accounts – in the balance sheet. It may look something like this:

Balance Sheet at 31 March 1995

Fixed assets	Freehold premises		£90,000
	Motor vehicles		£20,000
	Machinery and equipment		£25,000
			£135,000
Current assets	Stock	£75,000	
	Debtors	£60,000	
	Bank balance	£15,000	
		£150,000	
Current liabilities	Creditors	£85,000	
			£65,000
Net assets:			**£200,000**
Represented by: proprietor's capital account			£200,000

This is obviously a very simple balance sheet from which one might
draw the conclusion that the business was worth £200,000. It might
be, but drawing that conclusion from the above figures is much too
simple. It could be right if the business were to be closed down and
the assets sold for the figures stated. But that is not very likely.
Anyway, in our case we are not looking at the closure of business –
we just want to know what the business is worth. A business will
always be worth more if it is a going concern because it will have
another asset – that is called goodwill. Goodwill can be described
in a number of different ways but essentially it is the fact that
the business has regular customers, the ability to get more, and

therefore the opportunity to make profits. That is a valuable asset but it is rarely shown in the accounts. However, before looking at goodwill, let us examine a bit more the figures shown in the above simple balance sheet – just so that you have a clearer picture of the implications.

Starting with the freehold property; this is shown in the accounts at £90,000. However, is that what the property cost or is it the current market value? In any event, what is the current value; it may be worth selling the property at a huge profit and moving somewhere else. If there is no good reason why those particular premises should be used for the business a good deal of money could perhaps be released to pay a lump sum in the divorce settlement while not damaging the business significantly. The business could go somewhere else and, if necessary, rent premises without damaging its ability to earn profits apart from paying the rent, of course.

The motor vehicles, the machinery and the equipment might be old and worn out; or they may have been recently renewed; you should find out. The purchase of a fancy new sports car may not be viewed favourably in the divorce proceedings if at the same time it is claimed that there is no money available to make a lump sum payment. Alternatively, the machinery and fixtures may need replacing and funds may need to be set aside for this purpose. Remember also that in the event that the business were to close down the chances of being able to sell the machinery and equipment for anything like their balance sheet value are extremely unlikely. Similar comments would apply to stock because although the £75,000 would normally be the cost of the stock, trying to unload the whole of the stock at one go would almost invariably give rise to a loss. When a business closes down the debtors have a disagreeable reluctance to pay their debts – if the business is coming to an end, they no longer care about customer goodwill so if they can get away with not paying, they will. However, where the business is continuing the stock will be expected to earn its normal mark-up and the debts would probably be paid in full.

As far as the creditors of £85,000 are concerned it will be apparent that although in the ordinary course of events those creditors would be paid out of the continuing cash flow of the business, if the business were to come to an end there would be insufficient money in the bank to pay the creditors; even if all the debtors pay in full there would still be a shortfall. It would be necessary to sell the stock and get in all the debts before the creditors could be paid. This could put an unreasonable burden on the business and serious cash flow difficulties could emerge. This must not be overlooked but again, on the basis that the business will continue, the payment of the creditors does not look to be a problem.

The above rather general comments indicate that although this business looks as if it is worth £200,000 the reality may be something different. A wife who claimed an equal share of the business (for whatever reason) would be naïve to expect that the husband would or could just pay her £100,000 on the basis of these figures. Life, and business, are not like that. If the business comes to an end, the assets will not yield anything like as much as she thinks and the continuing earnings, out of which she may have been happy to receive some maintenance, will have been destroyed. On the other hand if the business is continuing where is the husband going to get the money to pay her? He only has £15,000 in the bank and he needs that, and more, to pay his creditors. He could borrow some perhaps but that might not be too easy. It would depend upon the true value of the property and what borrowings are already secured on it. In nearly all cases it will probably be in everybody's interests to keep the business going to provide the funds (or perhaps service the borrowings) for the divorce settlement.

So we should now return to goodwill. Remember that this is the opportunity to earn profits in the future. The value of the goodwill will obviously depend upon how large those profits are. If the business makes a profit of £20,000 per year and if the proprietor were to stop working in the business he would have to pay somebody £20,000 per year to run the business, the goodwill may not be worth very much. It would be worth something because of the possibility that the profits could be increased – but still it would not be worth very much. If however the business makes £30,000 per year and it would only cost £20,000 per year to get somebody to run the business in the absence of the proprietor, what is called a 'super profit' of £10,000 will arise and it is that which is the valuable element. Generally, goodwill is valued at a multiple of super profits and the multiple will depend upon the particular industry and the state of the economy and the market at the time. What would somebody pay for the right to make a profit of £10,000 per annum? If interest rates were 5 per cent this would be the return one would expect on an investment of £200,000; if interest rates were 10 per cent, the investment needed to produce £10,000 per annum would be only £100,000. This does not mean that the goodwill would be worth £200,000 or £100,000, because there is an obvious risk in buying a business? Why invest £100,000 in a business to get a return of £10,000 when you can get that from a building society or bank? The business might fail and you could lose all your money. However, it must be recognized that if you invest £100,000 and obtain a return of £10,000 you do have the opportunity to increase the profits of the business so as to increase the value of the goodwill in the future. You do not have the opportunity of enhancing the value of your investment when you put money in a building society. These risks must be taken into account when you decide what return you would like and many different judgements can be made in reaching the decision. The judgement is based on the security of the super profit and the return that you want from your investment.

Sometimes this calculation is expressed in terms of a price/earnings or PE ratio. This is mere jargon and it is another way of expressing the yield. It is found by dividing the profits (which are sometimes called earnings) by the price. To put this into mathematical form:

$$a = \text{the price} \qquad \frac{a}{b} = \text{the PE ratio}$$
$$b = \text{the earnings}$$

So, there are three factors and you will immediately see that if you have any two of them you can work out the third.

PE ratios are generally used in connection with shares in companies but the same concept can be used in connection with goodwill. If the super profit is £10,000 you need to decide how much you want to pay. You can do this by reference to the yield. Just putting your money on deposit might give you 7 per cent so perhaps you would say that you need an increased yield of 10 per cent if you were to take on the risks of buying a business. If £10,000 represents a yield of 10 per cent then the value of the goodwill would be £10,000 × 100/10 = £100,000. If you wanted a yield of 12.5 per cent the value of the goodwill would be £80,000. Expressing this in terms of a PE ratio is easy; you just convert the required yield to an index by turning it upside down.

$$\frac{12.5}{100} = 12.5\% \text{ which is the yield} \qquad \frac{100}{12.5} = 8 \text{ which is the PE ratio}$$

So a yield of 12.5 per cent is a PE ratio of 8. So if instead of saying you require a yield of 12.5 per cent you say that a PE of 8 is appropriate to this business, you end up with exactly the same figure.

I mention all this so that when considering what the business is worth and therefore what the party continuing the business can afford to pay, you do not get carried away with over-optimistic views about how much it is worth and how much it should be sold for (and therefore what a half-share is worth) or alternatively be blinded by figures put forward by the other side saying how little it is worth. It will usually be worthwhile to keep the business going and it is most unlikely that the courts would make an order which would deprive the husband of his livelihood. Killing the goose that lays the golden eggs (or any type of eggs) is never a good idea. Without the business the husband has no means of paying anything and that is not going to be in anybody's interests – unless you are after retribution and punishment in which case you should be reading another book.

There is also the possibility of the husband being able to raise money on the security of the business to pay a lump sum. One helpful rule of thumb would be to calculate how much the business earns by way of profit after an appropriate salary for the proprietor. That is what was called super profit in the above calculations. That super profit is the amount which the husband could afford to pay away in interest on money borrowing which would leave him in the same position as far as his earnings are concerned. A lump sum could therefore be borrowed of an amount which would give rise to interest on this amount – without seriously affecting the husband's livelihood. A lump sum of such an amount can be criticized on the grounds that it is too high – it gives the wife the whole of the value of the goodwill. Alternatively it can be credited as being too low because it leaves the husband with his ordinary profit and just deprives him of his super profit. Why should he end up comparatively unscathed if hardship is being shared between the parties? Which criticism is right naturally depends upon who is doing the criticizing.

However, look at the position objectively, and do check with the accountants that any borrowings which are raised will not become an insupportable burden. It is very easy to get carried away. It might look all right now but if interest rates go back up to their levels of only a few years ago, the cost of borrowing could double and be quite incapable of servicing. Borrowing money that cannot be repaid is probably the single most popular means of going bust.

If you do follow the route of a lump sum based on the security of the business, some very serious consideration has to be given to the tax position. A lump sum payable to the wife all from borrowed money will give rise to a lot of interest each year and it will be very important, and possibly crucial, that the husband receives a tax deduction for the interest he pays. If he does not get a tax deduction, he may not be able to afford to pay the interest.

In the simple case envisaged above where money is borrowed on the security of the business assets to pay a lump sum to the wife, the interest will certainly not be tax deductible. It does not matter that the loan is secured on the business premises or other business assets; what matters in connection with tax relief for interest paid, is what the money is spent on. It must be spent wholly and exclusively for the purposes of the business. It will not be; it will be spent on providing a lump sum to the wife in the divorce settlement.

You have to do it another way (and this is where the accountant will be able to help you structure the loan). Going back to the balance sheet illustrated above, there is an item called 'proprietor's capital account'. That is the amount which the business owes the proprietor. He can draw that money out at any time – at least he could if there was enough money in the bank to do so. What it means is that instead of there being a bank loan of £200,000, the proprietor is lending the business £200,000 of his own money, but of course he is not charging interest. However, there is no requirement that the proprietor should provide all or any of the finance for his business, although in purely practical terms this is often commercially inevitable.

Let us assume that Adam is the proprietor and he needs to pay Eve £100,000 as a lump sum in a divorce settlement. Using the above figures, if he withdrew £100,000 from the bank he would go overdrawn by £75,000. He would simply be withdrawing £75,000 of his own money so no tax would arise. He is now sharing the financing of the business between himself and the bank. But Adam would probably not want an overdraft at this level, it may be much more expensive than a business development loan which he would like to have instead. So he can now arrange the loan and pay the loan monies into the business bank account which he needs and will use for the purposes of the business. The loan interest would therefore be fully tax deductible. The loan he has taken out will have been advanced to the business to be used for the purposes of the trade and that makes the interest an allowable tax deduction.

While the loan remains outstanding both from the business to Adam and from Adam to the bank, the interest will continue to be tax deductible. If the loan is reduced the tax deduction for the interest will be correspondingly reduced. If at some later date Adam withdraws amounts from his capital account (beyond the normal withdrawal of his annual profits) his tax relief will be reduced because that will be treated as a recovery of part of the loan. It is crucial that this is done the right way round. If Adam were to borrow £75,000, put it into the business and then withdraw £75,000 for his own purposes, he would be treated as recovering the whole of the £75,000 and no tax relief would be available on that amount. By withdrawing the money first and then replacing it with borrowings, the borrowings are used for the correct purposes and are not recovered by Adam.

You may say this hardly makes any difference; the effect is just the same so why should the taxman deny you a tax deduction for the interest if you do it in a different order? In tax matters, most of the time what is important is not what you do but how you do it. Nearly doing it in accordance with the rules means that the taxman will nearly give you the relief – as a bookmaker will pay out on the horse you backed to win, not the horse which nearly won.

The above deals with the situation where the wife is to be paid a lump sum and the husband uses the business assets to obtain the money to pay her. What if the wife is a partner in the business and owns half of it? What happens when he buys her half of the share of the partnership business? Quite apart from the fact that the partnership does not have any money and will need to borrow in a tax efficient manner so that a tax deduction is obtained for the interest, the wife would be disposing of her interest in the partnership to her husband for capital gains tax purposes and her proceeds of sale could be taxable. The scope for disaster here is considerable. Just imagine borrowing money to pay the wife her share of the business without any tax deduction with any interest paid only to find that the amount you pay to her is then chargeable to tax in her hands.

Again it is not what you do but how you do it. Let us assume the same example as above; Adam and Eve are in partnership and their partners' accounts total £200,000 which coincidentally equals the value of the business. Adam could say that he will buy her half share for £100,000. He will borrow the money in the manner previously mentioned so that he gets a tax deduction for the interest but when he pays it to her, she would be selling her half interest in the partnership to him for £100,000. Assuming the business was originally started by them there would be no base value for capital gains tax and Eve would realize a gain of £100,000 on which the tax would be approximately £40,000. This would not be the case if this were to take place while they are still married and living together. If it were to take place in a tax year after the separation the capital gains tax exemption between husband and wife would not apply and the tax would become payable.

So they need to arrange matters differently. Instead of Adam buying Eve out, all he needs to do is arrange for Eve to withdraw the £100,000 standing to her credit in the partners' accounts, whereupon she can retire as a partner. She can withdraw this money without any tax implications – except that the business does not have enough money to enable her to do so. Borrowings would have to be raised and providing Adam goes through the same procedure as before (i.e. Adam borrows the money to put into the business), Eve can have her money out in a way which will cost her no tax at all; furthermore the interest on the borrowings will be tax deductible by Adam.

Family companies

Where the business is carried on by a company different considerations arise. That is because of the fundamental distinction that the business does not belong to the company's shareholders – the business belongs to the company and it is therefore the company that has all the value. The husband and wife just have shares in the company. That does not mean that the shares cannot be sold; they can, but you are dealing with a totally separate asset. If you are uncertain about companies and shares in companies you really need to have some advice from a lawyer or an accountant who can explain the company law position in some detail. Essentially a shareholder has no right to the assets of a company. He has the right to vote at meetings and to receive dividends; that is about it. If you have enough shares, for example 75 per cent, you can put the company into liquidation and obtain all the assets for yourself but that may not always be a good idea for the reasons that we have previously discussed; it may also create a lot of rather unattractive tax liabilities. Just because you are a shareholder does not mean that you can be a director and have any say in running the business. The shareholders appoint the directors but they are appointed by a simple majority (that is more than 50 per cent) so unless you have more than 50 per cent of the votes you cannot appoint yourself or anybody else as a director. If you have less than 50 per cent all you can do is to be a damned nuisance in the hope that you will receive some financial encouragement for not being such a nuisance. Otherwise, all you can do is vote at the meetings (and be outvoted by the others) and wait for your dividend.

You may wait a long time for a dividend. Whether or not a dividend is paid is a matter for the directors. They can pay a dividend at any time and they can recommend to the shareholders that they declare a dividend at a shareholders' meetings. However the shareholders cannot declare a dividend of more than the directors recommend. The law therefore puts the directors firmly in control of the payment of dividends.

So if the wife has say 40 per cent of the shares in the family company she is at a serious disadvantage if the husband is the controlling director. If he decides that there will be no dividend, there is not a lot she can do about it. However, she is not totally without power. If she can show that the company has adequate means to pay a dividend and that the decision not to pay one was not made by the husband in the best interests of the company, but for his own private purposes, she can create a real fuss. She can claim on good authority that one of the rights of being a shareholder is to share in the profitability of the company and to deprive a shareholder deliberately of their dividend is unfairly prejudicial to their interests. This is one of the grounds for seeking an order from the court that the company be wound up or alternatively for her shares to be purchased by one of the other shareholders. This prospect is not going to be viewed very favourably by the husband and drawing this point to his attention may well mean that dividends start to be paid.

But it is by no means as simple as this. Where there is an investment company with pots of money in the bank serving no real purpose, the position is reasonably clear. However, with a trading company the directors can always put up a good case for cash being required for the business, to meet the demands of creditors, as a cushion against a downturn in trade or to pay for new plant and machinery or for some planned expansion. Even if there is lots of money in the bank it will be a poor businessman who cannot think up compelling reasons why it would be unwise to deplete the company's resources by paying a dividend this year; maybe they will be able to pay a dividend next year (by which time of course he will have plans which make the payment of a dividend impossible that year as well). But do not let this put you off. Many husbands are poor businessmen and his reasons for not paying a dividend might be equally poor; this can give you added incentive and ammunition to encourage him to pay a sensible dividend.

The wife should not overlook the possibility that the company might actually owe her some money. If she is a director, the accounts may contain a director's loan account which will not necessarily be separately identified in the published accounts; it might be included generally in creditors. It will represent the money she put into the business and any remuneration which may have been voted to her, less, of course, amounts which have been paid to her. This is money which belongs to her and which she is entitled to ask for. If it causes cash-flow difficulties that is a pity; she is still entitled to it. A request for a copy of the director's loan account for the last three years might prove interesting – particularly if it is met with a look of panic in the eyes of the husband or his accountants.

Turning now to the value of the shares, let us look at a situation where a wife owns 30 per cent of the family company with the husband owning the other 70 per cent. We can look at the company's business and evaluate it in just the same way as an unincorporated business referred to above. You look at the assets, the profits earning capacity, the ability to pay his debts and everything else and let us assume you end up with the conclusion that the company's business is worth (say) £600,000. You may have gone to a lot of trouble to get to this stage but you are really only halfway there. This does not mean that the shares are worth £600,000. It is possible that the entire 100 per cent shareholding would be worth that amount but even that is doubtful. When you look at smaller shareholdings it is definitely not the case. A 30 per cent shareholding will not be worth £180,000 however much the wife would like it to be and you must understand this point if your thinking is not to go off the rails.

What asset does the wife have? It is not a proportion of the company's assets. It is a shareholding in the company which carries 30 per cent of the voting rights. That means she will be outvoted every time. That is not worth a great deal. She also has a right to 30 per cent of the dividends which may be paid, but that is dependent entirely on whether the directors decide to pay a dividend or not. If they do, she will receive 30 per cent of the dividend but if they do not she will receive nothing. That right is not worth a great deal either. If the company were to be liquidated she could get 30 per cent of the sale proceeds of all the assets but for all the reasons we have discussed before, that may be very much less than she thinks and there will be some tax liabilities to worry about as well. The company may be sold and she will then get 30 per cent of the sale proceeds. Unfortunately her shareholding does not entitle her to bring either of these courses of action about (unless she can get a court order in her favour on the grounds that she is being so unfairly prejudiced by the way the company is being conducted that the only satisfactory solution is for the company to come to an end and be liquidated – not a likely result in a trading company with a continuing business on which a number of people's livelihoods depend). Nor can she influence whether the company is sold. So those rights are not worth very much either.

All she has as a shareholder are these rights, nothing more, and in this type of case these rights are clearly not worth a great deal. Who would buy the shares on this basis? You will see that the possibility of finding a buyer for her shares in these circumstances is rather remote and finding a buyer at anything like what she regards as a reasonable price would be practically impossible. It is for these reasons that a minority shareholding is conventionally valued at a discount and the husband would apply a fairly heavy discount to reflect the small size of the holding. He may also seek to discount the value further by making reference to the fact that shares in a private company have no market; they cannot be bought and sold on the stock exchange like quoted public companies and therefore they are considerably less valuable than any other type of investment. He will have a whole list of reasons why her 30 per cent is worth very little. In these circumstances the husband has a very powerful case and the above arguments can be developed at great length to his advantage. Furthermore he will obtain a large number of expert share valuers to support him.

However, this is not the only point of view. The wife is not totally without arguments. She could quite reasonably suggest that the business was in reality run as a partnership even though it operated as a limited company. In that event it should be treated for valuation purposes as a partnership and therefore no discount should apply in respect of the minority holdings. This is a really good argument but it needs the facts to support it. If she does little work in the business, confining her interest mainly to a pride in her husband's business success, she can hardly claim that the business is really a partnership. On the other hand if she is involved a good deal in the business, not necessarily every day nor necessarily at the business premises like her husband, but makes a genuine and worthwhile contribution, possibly from home, that would be much more promising. She may not have the skills or professional qualifications to deal with the technical aspects of the business but she may spend lots of time dealing with administrative matters on the telephone, looking after the books, entertaining clients and generally attending to business-related matters at all hours, that is much more like a partnership and the argument looks very much stronger. It would not, of course, be a real partnership and the fact that she could not be a real partner would not really matter. The business would still be being carried on by the company but the argument here is that the business would be conducted in the same way as a partnership and the shares should be valued on that basis – that is, as a pro rata value of the business as a whole. This obviously makes a staggering difference to the value and with this in mind she might be well advised to participate as much as she can in her husband's business.

If we assume that one way or another a value of the wife's shareholding is agreed and the shares are being purchased by the husband, it is necessary to consider the capital gains tax position because this will represent a disposal for the purposes of the tax. If the transaction could be completed before the 5 April following the separation no problem would arise because the transfer would be treated as taking place at a value giving rise to neither gain nor loss irrespective of the actual price paid for the shares. Unfortunately however, this is rather unlikely. The parties will probably have been separated for some time and this opportunity will no longer be available. A capital gains tax liability is therefore likely to arise and something needs to be done about it.

Where the court orders a purchase by the husband, it may sound unfair for a liability to arise because the wife is only doing what the court has ordered. It was not a matter of choice, even though she may have been quite happy to do so. Unfortunately this makes no difference. It is a disposal and if a gain arises it will be taxable. The husband may be keen to help with this problem because if any tax arises he could end up having to provide her with funds to make up for the hole which has appeared in her resources by reason of the tax liability. They might therefore agree to arrange things in a more advantageous fashion.

Let us assume that Adam has 70 per cent of the shares in the family company and Eve has the other 30 per cent. As part of the financial arrangements Adam is required to purchase Eve's shares for £20,000. Eve's base cost for capital gain tax purposes is negligible so this £20,000 would all be a capital gain. The first £6,000 would be exempt leaving £14,000 taxable at 25 per cent i.e. a liability of £3,500.

Eve may be able to use the capital gains tax exemptions of the children to eliminate all or part of the gain. When she receives the money she may need to spend at least £15,000 on the maintenance, education and benefit of her two children over the next three years. Eve could therefore give 10 per cent of her shares to each of her children. The shares would have to be held by trustees because the children are infants but that would not matter; the trustees would simply hold the shares for the children absolutely. The trustees would acquire the shares at Eve's base cost because she could hold over the capital gain and when Adam buys 10 per cent from each of them for £6,666, Eve and the two children can all set their annual exemptions of £6,000 against their respective gains so that they each have a gain of £666 taxable at 20 per cent giving three lots of tax liabilities of £133; a total tax liability of £400 instead of £3,500. It would be very important indeed that Eve took great care to spend the children's money exclusively on their maintenance, education and benefit but with her solicitor's guidance this should not give rise to any problem.

Alternatively Eve might be able to take advantage of the new capital gains tax reinvestment relief which would enable her to reinvest any gain she makes on the disposal of her shares by buying shares in another company. She might be planning to start up a small business to support herself and her children and this would be a way of sheltering the gain possibly for a very long time. Let us assume that given the above circumstances, Eve sells her shares to Adam and realizes a gain of £20,000. She decides to use this money to start a business but instead of operating as a sole trader she decides to form Eve Limited and operate the business through a company. She puts her £20,000 into the company by way of share capital which enables her to claim reinvestment relief on her earlier disposal. Eve Limited need not use all the money immediately, it would just spend it as required, so the money would merely be in the company's bank account instead of her own. When eventually she sells Eve Limited the capital gain would arise, but there may be many years and there will be many opportunities to save the tax on that disposal.

Another alternative which may be attractive to Adam would be for the company to purchase its own shares. The company would need to have power to do so and to follow the proper procedures but the result could be that Eve receives the £20,000 from the company for her shares and the amount would be treated as a dividend from which tax at the basic rate had been paid. If she does not have any other income during that year (and remember that maintenance is not taxable in her hands) the amount received would not put her into the higher rate band. Her basic rate tax liability would be covered by the tax credit attaching to dividends and no tax would therefore be payable. She would receive the full £20,000 and the capital gains tax liability of £3,500 would be entirely saved.

Adam would be happy with this arrangement because although he has to pay advance corporation tax of approximately £5,000 (because the £20,000 would be treated as a dividend), he can deduct this £5,000 from the company's corporation tax liability on the profits for the year and he effectively gets his £5,000 back. He has not had to pay the money himself, the company has paid it all and he has not had to incur any personal debt. Furthermore, when the company purchases Eve's 30 per cent shareholding, the shares are cancelled and Adam's 70 per cent holding is thereby converted into a 100 per cent holding. Even if the figures were higher and Eve is pushed into the higher rate tax band by these arrangements, the advantages remain substantial.

There is of course a further alternative. The wife could simply retain her shares in the hope or expectation that the company will be sold in due course and she will receive full pro rata value for them. If she can afford to do so (and if there is a genuine prospect of a sale) this is probably the avenue which will maximize her sale proceeds.

8. The Effect of Bankruptcy

The effect of insolvency on maintenance

One of the many problems which will exercise the mind of any divorced wife in receipt of periodical payments is: what happens if he goes bankrupt? She might reasonably view the prospect with some anxiety and seek some protection from what looks like a potentially catastrophic situation.

Generally what happens when somebody goes bankrupt is that all their assets vest in their trustee in bankruptcy who uses them to pay the creditors. Unfortunately the value of the assets will be less than the amount due to the creditors – sometimes a great deal less – so where does this leave the wife who may be expecting to remain in the matrimonial home and to continue to receive periodical payments? The court cannot make any order about his capital assets; he does not have any – they have all gone to his trustee in bankruptcy.

Where the husband goes bankrupt after the divorce and while he is paying maintenance to the wife or child support for the child, the obligation to make these payments continues despite the bankruptcy. That is all very well in theory but he might not have the means to pay them; furthermore, he may well apply to the court to vary the maintenance payments or even suspend them if he simply cannot afford to pay. This could easily happen, for example, where an income payments order is made in the bankruptcy. However, there is no possibility of any variation being made to any child support payments.

If the husband stops paying the maintenance, the wife can still take action against him for the money because it is only the husband's capital which passes to his trustee in bankruptcy; his income does not and the wife could therefore seek an attachment of earnings order to meet the maintenance. Unfortunately, however, she will be competing with the trustee in bankruptcy who will be wanting as much of the husband's income as he can get to meet the claims of the creditors. The husband would have to be earning an awful lot of money to satisfy the Child Support Agency, the wife, the claims of the trustee in bankruptcy and of course the Inland Revenue who will still want their share of his earnings – and presumably he had in mind eating as well. The prospect of all these claims for the indefinite future encourages some husbands simply to give up and sink into the arms of the state.

How to protect the maintenance and the assets

The position with secured maintenance is different because the wife can look to her security if he stops paying the maintenance. The periodical payments may be made out of the fund in which case the payments would continue entirely unaffected by the insolvency; alternatively if the husband was making the payments himself, she would seek recourse from the amounts which are being held as security. It is, however, absolutely essential to ensure when considering secured maintenance (apart from all the other aspects mentioned in Chapter 3) that the arrangements cannot be set aside by the trustee in bankruptcy. Exactly the same considerations apply to lump sum settlements. There are two main areas of danger here. There is the 'transfer at an under value' provision of the Insolvency Act which means that if the husband has transferred amounts to his wife or to trustees to secure maintenance and goes bankrupt within two years, the assets will be recovered and the wife will lose out. If he goes bankrupt more than two years after the transfer, the trustee in bankruptcy will still be able to recover the assets if he can show that the husband was insolvent at the time he made the transfer or became insolvent as a result of doing so. However, after five years the trustee in bankruptcy has no claim.

The other danger area is where there has been 'a preference'; that is to say one creditor (namely the wife) has been preferred at the expense of the other creditors. The trustee in bankruptcy can attack a transaction as being a preference if it takes place within two years of the bankruptcy petition unless it can be shown that the husband was solvent at the time and did not become insolvent as a result of the transfer.

Because the solvency of the husband at the time of the transfer is so important, it is a very wise precaution to examine the husband's financial position very carefully at the time of the financial settlement. All his financial affairs will have been fully disclosed and his solvency can therefore be established – and preferably noted so as to frustrate any later attack by the trustee in bankruptcy.

Another useful protection is to demonstrate clearly at the time that the arrangements for setting up the maintenance or lump sum settlement were made in exchange for the wife giving up valuable claims which she might have made in the divorce proceedings. This is obviously much easier in the case of a lump sum settlement because that will usually be made in consideration for the wife relinquishing her right to periodical payments – or at least to a reduction in their amount. However, the figures need to make sense. What she is giving up ought to be broadly worth what he is transferring to her. It may be worthwhile to have a vigorous argument and lots of correspondence about it – and better still to have the result incorporated into the order. This might eliminate any suggestion being made later that it was a transfer at an undervalue. With secured maintenance it would be necessary to look at the circumstances more carefully to see whether the wife is really giving anything up. It may be that because of the element of security she was prepared to accept a smaller amount of maintenance or, perhaps as part of the secured arrangement, she relinquished her share in the matrimonial home – or at least gave up her claim to such a share. Whatever there is should be fully documented at the time as it may be much more difficult to reconstruct this later.

These considerations only apply to the assets of the husband who goes bankrupt; they obviously do not apply to assets which already belong to the wife by having been transferred to her or because they always belonged to her. For this reason a declaration under Section 17 MWPA 1882 confirming her interest in the property would be particularly valuable. However, it should not be overlooked that the vesting of the assets in the trustee in bankruptcy automatically severs any joint tenancy – so do not think that you have any protection by survivorship in the event that he dies before the property is sold. His half will go to the creditors – and not to you. An interesting additional point is that the wife may be able to claim additional sums if she has paid the mortgage since separation. There is some authority for this which is called the 'equity of exoneration' and would be good even against the trustee in bankruptcy.

Where the husband goes bankrupt before the ancillary relief order is made, the wife will face a very difficult problem. The husband would have no assets which the court can rely on to make a lump sum or property adjustment order. The only chance she has is a periodical payments order because although his capital assets will have been vested in his trustee in bankruptcy, his income will not have done so. However, the trustee in bankruptcy will also be seeking an income payments order for the benefit of the creditors and although the court will allow a minimum amount of income for the living expenses of himself and his family who are living with him, there is no allowance in respect of payments which may be needed to be made to a former wife. There may be precious little income left to pay any maintenance to her. The court might allow the payments to the creditors to be reduced to allow maintenance to be paid to the former wife but it is by no means certain that they will do so. This is very likely to leave her out in the cold.

The position with children is not the same because the Child Support Agency will not be inhibited by any bankruptcy proceedings from assessing the amount payable to the child and they will pursue it with all vigour. This, of course, is likely to make the position for the wife that much worse.

9. Wills

A will suffers from the inherent problem that the person who wrote it and who knows what it means is not there when you need them. A will only comes into operation on death and it has no effect whatsoever during lifetime. The person can change it out of all recognition without telling anybody and any number of surprises can therefore arise. Perhaps the biggest surprise is what happens if there is no will at all or, worse still, if the will is badly drafted. Mention has already been made of the possibility of all the money disappearing in professional costs during the divorce; anything which is left can easily be swallowed up by arguing over the will.

Intestacy

It may be best to start with the position where there is no will at all. In that case the deceased will be said to have died intestate. In that event the law states specifically who is to inherit the money of the deceased.

A recent survey by those interested in the subject revealed that 75 per cent of British adults do not have a will. There may be many reasons for this. They may feel that their estate is too small to warrant the trouble and expense of a will, or they may assume that by their doing nothing the surviving spouse will automatically inherit everything. This is possible – but only just. It would happen if there were no children or grandchildren, no parents, no brothers or sisters or nieces or nephews. Hardly very likely. Alternatively, it

may be one of those things that they are intending to get round to –
but not just at the moment.

The reasonably well informed will be aware that there are
statutory provisions dealing with the devolution of property on an
intestacy. However, they may not appreciate just how these rules
work or where their money may end up – and the tax implications
which can arise. If an individual dies intestate, the identity of those
who inherit his estate will vary, depending upon the size of the
estate and the configuration of the blood relations. In broad terms
it goes like this.

Survived by spouse and children

The spouse receives all the personal chattels, a statutory legacy of
£125,000 (plus interest), and a life interest only in half the residue
with the remainder going to the children. The children receive the
other half of the residue absolutely (or in trust while they are under
eighteen).

Therefore, if the estate is less than £125,000 the surviving spouse
will scoop the pool and there is no need to worry about anything
else. No inheritance tax arises because property passing to the
surviving spouse is exempt, and even if the surviving spouse is not
domiciled in the United Kingdom the amount would still be below
the threshold at which inheritance tax becomes payable. However,
if the estate is larger, problems begin to arise. If we were to assume
that the estate is worth £600,000, excluding personal chattels, the
estate would devolve thus:

Surviving spouse: statutory legacy	£125,000	*exempt from tax*
Life interest in half residue	£237,500	*exempt from tax*
	£362,500	
Children (absolutely or in trust)	£237,500	
Less allowance	£154,000	
Taxable	**£83,500**	*tax £33,000*
Total estate	**£600,000**	

Although the amount passing to the spouse would be exempt, that
passing to the children would be liable to inheritance tax, which,

after taking account of the nil rate band of £154,000, at today's rates would be approximately £33,000. Not too serious perhaps, but still pretty inconvenient, and as values increase so will the tax – and the rates may go up. However, the surviving spouse may be less concerned about the tax than that £237,500 of her husband's money has gone elsewhere. This might mean that she cannot maintain her standard of living without selling the matrimonial home.

Survived by spouse but no issue

In this case the surviving spouse still does not receive everything; the statutory legacy is increased to £200,000, but again the spouse receives absolutely only half the residue. The other half of the residue goes to the parents of the deceased – and if they are no longer alive, to the deceased's brothers or sisters. As before, only the amount passing to the spouse is exempt, the balance being chargeable to inheritance tax. This could be extremely irritating, because again not only does a tax liability arise, but the widow may find that a good part of her husband's money has gone to his brothers or sisters or, worse, to his nephews and nieces.

The position can be particularly awful if a tragedy occurs in the early years of marriage, before any children have been born. Let us assume that a rich husband and his younger (and less rich) wife are both involved in an accident; unless it can be shown that the wife died before the husband, his wealth will pass to her and almost immediately will pass to her parents. A single tragic accident could therefore cause the rich man's wealth to pass straight to his mother-in-law. Not necessarily a prospect he may have fully appreciated in his postnuptial bliss, and even worse difficulties would ensue if he had been the beneficiary of substantial *inter vivos* gifts from his parents as part of their tax planning arrangements – a significant shareholding in the family trading company, for example.

No surviving spouse

Where there is no surviving spouse, the estate of the deceased devolves in the following order. The first to qualify takes the lot, and all those in the same class share it all equally.

a) Issue.
b) Parents.
c) Siblings and the issue of deceased siblings.
d) Siblings of the half-blood and issue of a deceased half-sibling.
e) Grandparents.
f) Uncles and aunts and issue of any deceased uncles and aunts.
g) Uncles and aunts of the half-blood and, if deceased, their issue.
h) The Crown.

It should be noted that all the above are blood relations, so step-relatives and in-laws will find themselves totally excluded, however close to the deceased they might otherwise have been. A first cousin twice removed, or some distant niece, will have a claim, whereas a beloved stepsister or stepmother will not.

None of the persons in the above list are exempt beneficiaries, so tax will arise on the estate. The deceased may not have much cared about inheritance tax; he may suggest, for example, that his children or othes will do very nicely out of his money, but it would be a strange testator (or rather non-testator) who would prefer his money went to the Inland Revenue rather than his children. Furthermore, by failing to make a will he may deprive the heirs of some valuable opportunities to save inheritance tax as well as capital gains tax and income tax. A deed of variation is a useful way to solve a number of these tax difficulties, but a deed of variation is not always a practical possibility – and is much less effective than a disposition by will.

The position would of course be very much more serious if the deceased was enjoying a relationship unrestrained by the heavenly chains of matrimony. In these circumstances the partner, companion, friend, cohabitee or what you will receives nothing under the intestacy rules. That could be entirely contrary to the wishes of the deceased, but that is too bad; he should have made his wishes known. If there are children of this union, they would be entitled to something but the surviving parent would not and although he or she may be able to make a claim to the estate under the Inheritance (Provision for Family and Dependants) Act 1975, there is no guarantee that such a claim would succeed – particularly if the deceased is the female partner, because the other may not be able to claim that he was being maintained by the deceased at the time of her death. Furthermore, no exemption from inheritance tax would of course be available. This can lead not only to financial and tax catastrophe, but to a certain loss of harmony between those who inherit at the companion's expense.

It is even more difficult for those who live in Scotland because the Act does not apply there and there is no entitlement under any similar provision. This puts the cohabitee in a precarious financial position. The only sensible answer is for the couple to ensure that the survivor is properly protected and provided for in the event of the death of one of the parties.

The essential point here is that if somebody dies without making a will, the persons receiving the money may be very different from those the deceased thought would benefit. Add to this the clear tax and administration disadvantages and you have the makings of a real disaster, which may not be capable of being repaired.

Where a will exists

So much for the position if there is no will. If there is a will it can be extremely important when it was made because marriage automatically revokes an existing will unless the will is made in contemplation of the marriage. It is not enough to be aware of the terms of your spouse's will; you need to know the date when it was executed. This is rather a sensitive enquiry to make at the best of times and perhaps rather hostile at a time when the marriage is in danger of coming to an end. However, it can be extremely serious. Just think of a couple who marry after having cohabited for some time. During the period of cohabitation a will may have been made by one party leaving the home or other assets to the other party. In due course they get married, the marriage founders and the husband (let us assume that it is he who made the will) dies. There is no valid will on his death. His earlier will, which no doubt they were both relying on as remaining effective, was revoked on the occasion of their marriage and the wife could therefore be in the most serious difficulty. She may be able to make a claim under the Inheritance (Provision for Family and Dependants) Act 1975, but that may be a long way from what they had both intended.

An alternative situation would be where one spouse looks at the will of the other and sees that it says that everything passes to the surviving spouse but fails to notice the date on the will, which had been drawn up during the existence of a previous marriage. Again, remarriage would have revoked this will and the deceased would have died intestate. She may end up with nothing.

Unfortunately, just to make life difficult, the same does not apply on divorce. Divorce does not revoke the will. The will continues except that it will operate as if the former spouse had died immediately before the divorce so as to exclude them from any benefit under the will; similarly any appointment of the former spouse as executor or trustee under the will will be ineffective. That is fine unless the spouse would have become entitled to the residue or a share of the residue. In that case there will be a partial intestacy and you are back to the list referred to above on page 148. The former spouse will not be able to benefit under the intestacy because a divorced spouse is not in the list of beneficiaries. They would have to rely on the Inheritance (Provision for Family and Dependants) Act 1975 but in these circumstances it would be almost impossible to satisfy the conditions. A different problem would arise if death occurs before the divorce has taken place or where a decree of judicial separation is in effect. In these cases the entitlement of the surviving spouse will continue – no doubt against the wishes of the deceased.

There is another problem that can arise. Let us assume that Adam expects his estate to be approximately £200,000 on his death, made up as follows:

Matrimonial home	£150,000
Savings	£50,000
	£200,000

He leaves Eve, his wife, his interest in the house and a legacy of £20,000 with the rest (the residue) being shared equally among his two children and his old school.

If they divorce, the effect will be dramatic. The legacy to Eve will lapse and the estate will then be divided equally between his two children and his old school. He had in mind that his school would get approximately £10,000 but now it will get £66,666. This will be a desperate problem for the children who will have to sell the house to meet the obligation to the school; the cash in the estate is not enough to satisfy their one-third.

Mutual wills

There is considerable misunderstanding about mutual wills. They are to be distinguished from reciprocal wills. Reciprocal wills arise where the husband leaves all his assets to the wife and the wife leaves all her assets to the husband. These wills just reflect the wishes of each party and that is all. Mutual wills are very different indeed and can create a binding obligation to overcome the normal rule that a will can be revoked at any time. Mutual wills are a species of constructive trust and arise where two people (not necessarily husband and wife) agree how their assets should devolve on their death and each executes a will conditional upon the other executing a will on similar terms. An example would be that the husband leaves his money to X in his will on condition that the wife leaves her money to Y (or perhaps to X) in her will. Each will is made in the knowledge of the other and on condition that the other will do so. This creates a trust and although it can be changed during lifetime, it cannot be changed without informing the other party (so that they are released from their obligations and can change their will if they want to). After the first death the will of the survivor cannot be changed. It becomes irrevocable. On the first death the survivor is bound by trust law to adhere to the terms of their will to discharge the obligation to the deceased whose will can obviously not be changed.

10. Cohabitation

One way of steering clear of all this divorce business is not to get married in the first place. That may seem attractive to some, perhaps those who do not want the responsibility or the dependence which is necessarily involved in marriage, and who prefer to affirm their commitment on a daily basis. Others view the institution of marriage as legalized prostitution and want no part of it.

Whether or not one takes an extreme view of the matter, nobody is obliged to get married; certainly not these days, although society and the law have not yet caught up with this modern approach. The law imposes various rights and responsibilities on those who are legally married, and by getting married you become entitled to, and are bound by, those obligations. If you want to be married, but do not want to take on the responsibilities which go with it, that is too bad; you must accept them. Similarly if you want the protections afforded to a spouse, but do not want to get married, that is too bad as well. In short, if you want the rights and obligations, then get married; if not, then don't.

For better or worse, to coin a phrase, the law does little to encourage cohabitation. The principle seems to be that marriage is an important stabilizing influence in our society and for cohabitants to gain rights similar to those of spouses would undermine the institution of marriage. Those rights and responsibilities should not be thrust upon them. They should be free to choose – and free to accept the consequences.

Unfortunately this freedom is not always available, where, for example, marriage is not possible; perhaps one party is already married and unable to obtain a divorce. In that case the rights which are imposed on a married couple by the law and which are not imposed on cohabitants can be created by the couple themselves by contract.

Financial implications

The purpose of this chapter is not to discuss the rights and wrongs of marriage or cohabitation but to examine the financial implications of failing to marry in the first place. If you are not married you get very little protection from the legislation if the relationship comes to an end. There is not much chance of any financial settlement at all. The same is not true if there are children. The children of the union are protected in practically the same way as if they had been born in wedlock. The absence of a marriage may have an effect on the court's discretion over custody but otherwise the position is broadly unchanged. There can be some wider effects – for example, the existence of children can have an inhibiting effect on the proposed sale of the house where they all live. However, it is not the cohabitant who obtains rights, but the children.

It is important to emphasize that cohabitation is not penalized in the sense that rights are diminished or taken away; it is just that cohabitants, unlike their married counterparts, do not have any extra rights by reason of their cohabitation. However, married couples are not the only ones who buy property in which to live together and when the relationship breaks down cannot agree who actually owns it, or in what proportions. The wife (and still more so the cohabitant) who allows the property to be in the sole name of their partner represents a triumph of hope over common sense. So where the cohabitant has contributed to the home, the same principles apply as with anybody else about whether an interest in the property has been created. Those rights do not arise under the Married Women's Property Act or similar legislation but they can still arise under the doctrine of constructive trusts. A constructive trust arises or is imposed by the law where property is held by one person and justice and fairness dictate that somebody else should have an interest in it. Examples would be if there is an express declaration that the property is held jointly or if both parties have provided part of the purchase price or even from the common intention of the parties. This is a well-known and long-established principle but it has nothing to do with cohabitation; it is a central plank of the law of property.

What does all this mean in practice? It means that the cohabitant who is claiming an interest in the property will have to prove a contribution to the acquisition of the house, on similar principles to that which would apply to a spouse making a similar claim under S17 Married Women's Property Act 1882. But there are problems. A husband has a legal obligation to maintain his wife, and so any contribution by the wife to the household can more easily be regarded as an indirect contribution to the property acquired during the marriage. No such obligations exist on a cohabitant so contributions to the household are more likely to be regarded as merely her share of the running expenses and not a contribution to the acquisition of the property. A striking example of this occurred in 1984 where a couple had lived together as man and wife for nineteen years. She gave up her job and devoted herself to looking after their two children. The property was in the man's sole name and she was not treated as having made any contribution to its acquisition. What is required is a financial contribution, or at least a contribution in money's worth such as work in helping to build the house; without it, no matter how meritorious her conduct she will not be entitled to any share in the property.

Even if the cohabitant cannot establish an entitlement to part of the property in this way, there is always the equitable doctrine of estoppel. Lawyers love estoppel. It is their way of saying 'CAN'T'!

What it means is that if one party to the relationship spends some money or does something to her detriment because the other says, or leads her to believe, that she owns or will be given an interest in the property, he will be 'estopped', that is, prevented from denying that she has an interest, even if he is the sole legal owner. The court will therefore order that she owns part of the property – or possibly all of it, depending on the circumstances.

One should also look at the possibility of an agreement existing between the parties that they should own the house jointly, notwithstanding it is in his sole name. There may not be a written agreement (if there is, few problems will arise) but an agreement would be implied by the conduct of the parties. If, for example, a couple lived together on the understanding that on the death of one party or on a breakdown of the relationship, the other would be able to continue to live there or have a share of the sale proceeds, the courts may well insist that this agreement is adhered to. It would, however, need some evidence to support such an agreement because cohabitation would not necessarily be enough on its own. That could occur for any number of reasons, not least love and affection for the other party, without any agreement regarding the sharing of property rights.

On the other hand it is not unusual for the cohabitants to enter into an agreement to prevent the acquisition of property interest and to confirm that the property is owned exclusively by one party. The document would state that the property is owned by one party and acknowledges that the cohabitant has no interest in the property and that this will not be affected by the occupation. It would go on to provide that the cohabitant has specific rights of occupation, that the legal owner would pay all the mortgage repayments but that both parties would share in the common household expenses. This would prevent the cohabitant obtaining an interest in the property but it gives rise to a number of emotional and social considerations beyond the scope of mere money and it may be regarded as sensible for legal advice to be sought before entering into any agreement which would deprive the cohabitant of legal rights. It may well be thought that to start a relationship with a legal document confirming that property is not to be shared is hardly an expression of confidence in the relationship.

Inheritance and wills

One area where a cohabitant can obtain some relief or benefit is in the event of the death of the other partner. However, this is by no means guaranteed. If one party to a relationship dies and does not leave the other adequately provided for in his will serious financial hardship can arise – made substantially worse by the tax implications. The most obvious example would be where there is no will and the deceased's estate therefore passes under the rules of intestacy to various members of his family and the unmarried partner gets nothing. In these circumstances the survivor can make a claim under the Inheritance (Provision for Family and Dependants) Act 1975 for maintenance out of the estate but the position is not at all straightforward. It is necessary for the cohabitant to prove that immediately before her partner's death she was being wholly or partly maintained by him.

If those who would otherwise be entitled to the deceased's money are to be denied part of their inheritance, the legal requirements have to be very carefully and precisely satisfied. This may sound harsh but the criticism should not be directed at the legislation. The fault or blame, if there is any, lies at the door of the deceased who failed to make adequate provision for his partner – the easiest way of doing so being by will. It is the same old point; the absence of a marriage means that the couple take themselves outside the legal consequences of marriage. By choosing not to have those rights and responsibilities but to regulate their affairs themselves they assume an obligation to do so. If they choose to regulate their affairs themselves and then fail to do so, one might say they are the authors of their own misfortune.

For this relief it is essential that the cohabitant was dependent on the deceased immediately before his death. This does not necessarily mean just at that instant and at no other time; a settled period of dependence has to be established but it must continue right up until death. Ceasing to be maintained by the deceased by reason of a change in circumstances just before the death could mean that relief would be completely denied. Furthermore, if the couple live together, each making an equal contribution towards the household, neither would be dependent on the other and therefore neither would be entitled to claim anything from the other's estate.

Entitlement to maintenance

Assuming that the survivor can prove that she was being maintained by the deceased immediately before the death, the amount of the award under the Inheritance (Provision for Family and Dependants) Act 1975 will not merely be nominal – just enabling her to survive at some low level. It will be an amount enabling her to live as decently and comfortably as is reasonable under the circumstances. This is not, however, a matter that you can hope to pursue profitably on your own; professional advice will be essential. (There are proposals for change in this area. At the time of writing the Law Reform (Succession) Bill proposes that a cohabitant can also qualify for provision under the Act without needing to show dependency. If these changes are enacted the cohabitant will merely need to show that during the whole of the two-year period ending immediately before death, they were living together in the same household as husband and wife.)

A particularly difficult problem arises when the female partner is genuinely dependent on the male partner but they own their home equally. In the event of his death she is protected and can claim against his estate for the above reasons; if however she were to die, he would not be entitled to any part of her estate because however close and settled their relationship, he would not be dependent upon her. Accordingly, her share in the house would pass to her family and it would either have to be sold or he would need to buy it from them. This position is exacerbated by the possibility of a tax charge arising from the absence of the spouse exemption; this is dealt with in more detail below. One useful precaution in circumstances such as these is to ensure that all properties are held as beneficial joint tenants and not as tenants in common. It will be remembered from Chapter 5 that this means on the death of one joint owner, the other becomes automatically entitled to the whole of the property and it does not fall to be dealt with under the will of the deceased or under the intestacy rules if there is no will. No dependence or any other conditions are necessary; it is just the legal effect of holding property in this manner. This does not improve the tax position, but at least the survivor keeps the property.

Pre-nuptial and cohabitation agreements

These may sound the same but they are not. A cohabitation agreement is a contract drawn up between individuals who live together, intended to regulate their relationship in the same (or perhaps a different) way as that which would apply if they were to marry. By doing so they provide themselves with the protection which the law automatically provides by reason of the marriage. (That should not be too surprising. A marriage is not just a spiritual undertaking, it is a legal contract as well. A cohabitation agreement can therefore be looked at as the legal contract without the spiritual bit.) A pre-nuptial agreement on the other hand is an agreement entered into before marriage but with marriage expressly in contemplation. A pre-nuptial agreement is therefore likely to be void if the marriage does not take place, although it could be drafted to be effective even if the marriage is called off.

Cohabitation agreements are not new. There are reported cases centuries old where the courts have enforced a promise made by a man to make financial provision for his partner. The disadvantages faced by the cohabitant when the relationship comes to an end have been mentioned above; these can be avoided by a cohabitation agreement which says that if the relationship ceases one shall pay the other a lump sum or periodical payments. That would be enforceable just like any other contract but it also suffers from the same disadvantage – it is only any good if there are funds to pay. This is not a problem confined to unmarried couples.

Some cohabitation agreements are designed to achieve exactly the opposite objective – each undertakes that they will have no claim on the assets of the other. The reasons for this can be many and various – not just an unwillingness to share their winnings in the National Lottery. One or other might have been married before or otherwise have children or family whom they want to benefit from their money without any claims from the other party. Alternatively, one party may be very rich and anxious lest the motives of the other have been or will become confused by the wealth. As far as the house is concerned it was mentioned above that the couple may prepare a document to show that the cohabitant does not have a share in the property. The wording for such a document can now be found in books of legal precedents which set out the obligations regarding the mortgage and contributions to the outgoings.

A variation of a pre-nuptial agreement is the pre-nuptial settlement which is often utilized where one party is wealthy and (sometimes from parental pressure) does not want to place all the wealth at the effective disposal of the new spouse. The idea would be that the wealthy fiancée settles the assets on herself for life so that during her lifetime she receives the income only and after her death her husband is entitled to the income only; after his death the capital would pass to their children or to some other member of her family. This cuts her new husband out completely except in respect of the income and that is often regarded as safe enough. If she requires capital, she can ask the trustees to provide it – but they will often be experienced professional advisers who will be able to guide her as appropriate to appreciate the financial consequences of her request for capital.

This sounds satisfactory from a financial point of view but it does not do a great deal for the family harmony. The new husband will feel at best disappointed that his wife's family have forced her into making such a settlement (she, of course, would never have thought it necessary) which is a vote of confidence against him; at worst it can poison the relationship between husband and wife and create the very problems it was designed to avoid.

A difficulty with a pre-nuptial settlement is that it is one of the areas in which the court can interfere when deciding the financial provision on a divorce. It will be remembered that one of the orders open to the court on an application for ancillary relief is the value of any settlement made by the other party in contemplation of the marriage.

To avoid all the problems, a wise parent might wheel their wealthy offspring along to their lawyer's office immediately they reach the age of eighteen for advice on the advisability of having all their assets appropriately settled long before any prospective suitor arrives on the scene. In this way the possibility of offence being taken by the spouse in due course would be eliminated and the ability of the court to rearrange the settlement for the benefit of the spouse on a subsequent marriage and divorce would similarly be diminished.

Presumption of marriage

One point which can prove useful in some circumstances and which should not be entirely dismissed, is marriage by repute. There is a general presumption of law that the parties are married if they live together as husband and wife. As with any presumption, it is capable of being rebutted but in these circumstances the contrary must be clearly proved. This is unlikely to be of interest to those who as a deliberate personal statement decide not to be married, but in some cases it could prove helpful in providing a cohabitant with grounds for financial relief (or in saving some tax), simply on the grounds that there is no evidence to rebut the presumption of a legal marriage.

Cohabitation after divorce

Where a former or separated spouse in receipt of maintenance cohabits with a new partner, this can give grounds for the original maintenance order to be varied. It will be necessary to show that the cohabitation is of a permanent nature and, more importantly, that the new partner is making a financial contribution to the other. The former husband will not be released entirely from his obligations to pay maintenance to his former wife but her needs may obviously have been reduced. This is unsatisfactory for the husband because he may know that if his ex-wife remarried his obligations to pay maintenance to her would cease; he may feel she is deliberately avoiding remarriage so that she can continue receiving maintenance from him. The courts have expressed some sympathy with this view suggesting that she should not be in a better financial position just by cohabiting with a new partner in a stable relationship than if she remarried. However, the situation is never that simple.

Looking at the position from the wife's perspective, she may be cohabiting with a new partner and be in receipt of maintenance from her former husband but she may have no intention of remarrying. She may value her independence including her financial independence and she may not be avoiding remarriage simply as a means of getting more money from her husband. She may enjoy the attention of her new partner without any wish for a permanent relationship for which he may not be at all suitable. For her to lose her financial independence by reason of the friends she may choose for the time being would be harsh indeed and would be an unreasonable restraint on her personal freedom.

What, however, if the husband who is paying maintenance remarries or cohabits with a new partner of substantial means? Should that give grounds for the former wife to claim an increase in her maintenance? It is obviously not fair for the new partner to have to contribute directly or indirectly to the maintenance for the former wife, but the fact remains that her contribution to the household means that the husband has more of his funds available to support his former wife. A technical problem arises here, however, because it may be very difficult to obtain details of the cohabitants' means; without evidence of these means they will not be able to be taken into consideration.

It is possible to get all these matters sorted out at the time of the divorce so that neither side can go back later and claim more or seek to pay less because of changing financial circumstances. Unfortunately, although that is possible, the conflicting interests of the parties mean that it is most unlikely any agreement will be made. However, for the alert spouse who sees the opportunity there is obviously some advantage to be gained.

Taxation

It will be apparent from the first half of this chapter that those who decide to share their lives free from the manacles of matrimony should do so with their eyes open to the financial consequences. They should also be aware of the tax implications because although there are some disadvantages, there are also some real advantages; where the balance of advantage lies will depend upon the precise circumstances of the parties.

Income tax

Since the introduction of independent taxation of husbands and wives in 1990 the income tax disadvantages to which wives were subject to for many years no longer exist. These disadvantages were significant because all the income of the married woman was deemed to be the income of her husband and taxed at his rates without any recognition of her allowances or her lower rate bands. This had been ameliorated by an opportunity to have her earnings taxed separately but unearned income was always taxed on the husband. This was all swept away in 1990 and spouses are now taxed entirely separately – well, almost. There are a number of obscure provisions, mainly designed to prevent tax avoidance, where a husband can still be taxed on income accruing to his wife – an example would be the income from a trust where his wife is a beneficiary. Clearly those provisions (and there are lots of them – but much too boringly technical to be examined here) will have no application to cohabitants.

There used to be a married man's allowance but this is now called the married couple's allowance of £1,720 per annum. Fiscal emancipation is not yet complete because this is only given to the husband, and although any unused allowances can be transferred to his wife, this opportunity does not exist the other way round. None of this applies to cohabitants. Obviously a man will not be entitled to the married couple's allowance unless he is married. However, if there are children the loss of this allowance will not matter because the same relief will be obtained in another way; this is the additional personal allowance for children which is the same amount. There was a time when if there were two children each party could obtain the additional personal allowance for one child, but now where an unmarried couple are living together as husband

and wife they can only obtain one such allowance. Quite what is meant by 'living together as husband and wife' is not clear and one might choose to argue about what this means. Do they have to live together pretending to be husband and wife or is it enough to live together in a deliberate unmarried state but otherwise in the manner in which a married couple would live – sharing all the facilities of the household, meals, bathroom, bedroom, etc? But how far does this go? With the relief amounting to only £1,720, and only worth £258 in tax, the argument is likely to stop long before it gets interesting.

One might have thought that being unmarried, each party would be treated separately for the purposes of interest relief on the mortgage of their main residence. After all each party can have a separate exemption for their main residence for capital gains tax so why should there not be a separate £30,000 mortgage limit for each party? Unfortunately not; it was removed in 1988 and to make matters worse there is no opportunity given to unmarried couples to elect for the mortgage interest paid by one to be deductible against the income of the other. Cohabitants will still be entitled to the relief on the interest for the first £30,000 of the mortgage on their home, but the strict conditions will apply. Only the party paying the interest can obtain the tax relief and that party must be the one responsible for the mortgage and must have an interest in the house. If they jointly own the property and are jointly responsible for the mortgage, each must pay half the interest if full tax relief is to be obtained – and only then against their respective incomes. If one party has little or no income, and therefore pays no tax, the value of the tax relief will be greatly reduced. This is irritating more than a serious problem because the amounts involved are not very large since the relief is now given at the rate of only 15 per cent, but it is a pity to lose out by failing to arrange things in the best way.

Another tax saving opportunity which is denied to cohabitants is the ability to limit the tax payable on income from jointly owned property. A married couple holding assets jointly, such as a portfolio of shares, a building society account or a rented property can elect to be taxed on the income from the assets on the basis of the proportion in which they own the assets. For example, they may own the asset two-thirds:one-third but they can be taxed on the income equally whatever their respective interest in the underlying asset. This provides a valuable opportunity to divide assets between married couples in the most suitable fashion to keep the income tax to a minimum without necessarily affecting the rights to the underlying capital. This can be of real value if the income is high. Unfortunately this opportunity is denied to cohabitants.

Capital gains tax

Although for income tax purposes, cohabitation might reasonably be regarded as disadvantageous, at least compared with the tax position of a married couple, capital gains tax provides some advantages. The most significant advantage available to an un-married couple is the entitlement to the exemption from tax for any gain made on their only or main residence. A married couple are entitled to only one exemption between them and if they have more than one property they must elect which one is to benefit from the exemption. However, this restriction has no application for coha-bitants and they can have two exempt properties. This is not necessarily so wonderful a result as it might seem because, as explained in Chapter 3, the same result can be achieved by the use of a trust, but one should not complain about the availability of a relief. However, it is not entirely straightforward and you must take care.

Let us assume that the couple live in a house in London and have a house in the country. If he owns one and she owns the other each can treat their own property as their only or main residence. After all, if each owns only one property, each can say that the property is their only residence. They may live somewhere else part of the time but only as a guest of the other person. However, what if they have both contributed to the acquisition of one of the properties by reason of the doctrine of constructive trusts; in that case she could perhaps claim an interest in that property. If she owns an interest in the property as a matter of law, that is a point which can be taken by the Inland Revenue as well. The law applies to everybody.

Accordingly, the Inland Revenue might say that she has a house in the country but that is not her only or main residence; she also has an interest in the property in London which is in fact where she lives most of the time so they will apply the exemption on the London property, leaving the country house fully chargeable. Her interest might be very small indeed but if it exists at all it means that the country house will not be the only residence and therefore not automatically exempt.

This would be obviously very inconvenient and the problem is that an argument is most unlikely to be raised until after it is too late. However, providing you see it coming, the problem can be solved.

If this could be a danger, she could elect to treat the house in the country as her main residence and to leave the (possibly very small) interest in the London property chargeable. This election can be made when there is more than one property which could possibly qualify as the main residence and must be made within two years of acquiring the second property. If therefore there is a danger of acquiring an interest in a residence inadvertently for these reasons, care must be taken to make the election in good time.

Now let us consider the position of the couple who own both properties jointly. Each owns a half-interest in two properties – but that does not add up to one whole property and the private residence exemption will only be given on one property. So each will be entitled to the exemption on their half of one of the properties (they can choose which one by making an election) but their respective half-interests in the other house will not be exempt.

For a couple in this situation, the solution is not to exchange their property interests. That would be a disaster. The effect would be that he would be transferring a half-interest in one property to her in return for her transferring a half-interest in the other property to him. Transfers between a married couple are treated as neutral in tax terms giving rise to no capital gains tax implications but this rule does not apply to unmarried couples. Each would be treated as if they had sold their respective half-interests in the property to the other at market value and any capital gain which then existed would crystallize. So by trying to save the tax, they would in fact create it. However, the solution would be for each to make an election for a different property before they exchange their interests, as explained below.

In 1990 Adam and Eve bought a flat in London in their joint names which they use as their main residence. In September 1994 they bought a house in the country, again in their joint names, which they use at weekends and holidays. In August 1996 when both properties are standing at a substantial capital gain they realize that the capital gains tax position is unsatisfactory and decide to exchange their interests. Before September 1996 Adam elects for the London flat to be treated as his main residence for capital gains tax purposes and Eve elects that the country house is her main residence. Adam then transfers his half-share in the London flat to Eve and the gain arising is exempt, as this is his main residence. Eve transfers her half-interest in the country house to Adam and her gain is exempt for the same reason. Adam now owns the country house completely and Eve owns the London flat completely. They now both have one property only and no election is necessary.

What, however, if they learn of the need to make such elections too late – that is, after the two-year period has expired? That looks like a serious problem but the answer is somehow to recover the right to make the election. The acquisition of a third property would mean that the time limit for the election of all three properties would be restarted but this is perhaps a rather dramatic means of regaining the opportunity of making an election. More useful would be for them to transfer their interest in one property (the property which is in fact their main residence) to a trust for their own benefit. That would be a disposal for capital gains tax purposes but the gain would be exempt because it would be a gain on the exempt property. By doing this, the time limit would start again as far as the election is concerned and they could then elect for the other property to be their main residence.

The permutations here are practically endless; the important thing is to realize that there are potential problems with the application of the private residence exemption and to make sure that these problems are solved before any gain arises.

Married couples of course have no such problems because of the rule that transfers of assets between spouses are disregarded. Married couples can therefore arrange their assets much more easily to get the best tax position but unfortunately they cannot qualify for two private residence exemptions.

It is for this reason that it is much more difficult for cohabitants to take advantage of the annual exemption of £6000. The exemption applies equally to married couples as it does to unmarried couples; each individual is entitled to make £6000 on gains each year tax free. However, that is fine if both parties have assets on which gains of this level can be made. If the gains are likely to be made by one party, it is helpful to be able to transfer the opportunity of making a gain to the other. Married couples can do this with ease. A transfer of an asset pregnant with gain to the other spouse will be treated as being transferred at a value which gives rise to no gain so that any subsequent disposal by the donee can benefit from the exemption. Unfortunately, this does not apply to cohabitants because any transfers between unmarried couples are deemed to take place at market value. Accordingly the gain crystallizes in the hands of the donor and the donee is therefore unable to make a gain at all. The only exception to this rule is where the asset qualifies for hold-over relief in which case it can be transferred to the other party at a price which gives rise to no gain; the donee can then realize the gain and benefit from the exemption. However there is a very limited class of asset to which hold-over relief applies – mainly business property or shares in trading companies which rather limits the opportunities for this type of planning.

Inheritance tax

It is in the area of inheritance tax that the position of cohabitants is potentially catastrophic. What if one of them dies? We have looked earlier at the position where one party dies without making adequate provision for the other and that property testamentary arrangements ought to be made by both parties. However, even if that is done, it does not help the tax position. Where a husband dies, that part of his estate which passes to his spouse is exempt from inheritance tax. It may enhance her estate and give her an inheritance tax problem in due course. But at least she does not have to fork out a large sum of money by reason of his death. The exemption is designed to deal with that problem. However, the exemption does not apply to unmarried couples and the chances of a serious tax liability arising are therefore very high. Take for example the position of Adam and Eve who live together in Adam's London flat worth £300,000. They jointly own a holiday home in Cornwall worth £120,000 and Adam has savings of £80,000. They have two children and Eve does not work. Adam dies and the inheritance tax liability on his death is approximately £112,000. Just at the time when Eve needs them most, the savings will all go in tax and one of the houses will have to go. There may be some life assurance, but that might have been just enough to pay off the mortgages.

The figures will of course be different in every case but the above illustrates the serious problem facing the surviving cohabitant who can find themselves in a position where they have to pay an unacceptably high tax liability simply because of the absence of the spouse exemption. There is no easy answer to this. What needs to be done is for steps to be taken so that on either death the tax is kept to a minimum and that adequate life assurance cover is taken out to protect the survivor from serious financial harm. In this example it would be sensible for the combined assets of £500,000 to be divided equally between the parties. A helpful point with regard to properties owned jointly is that individually the half-interests are worth somewhat less than 50 per cent of the whole because of the unmarketability of a half-interest in a property. A discount of at least 10 per cent can be deducted in the valuation and sometimes a good deal more. So by evening out their estate the position would be:

	Adam	Eve
London house	135,000	135,000
Holiday house	54,000	54,000
Investments	40,000	40,000
	£229,000	**£229,000**

Whoever dies first, the tax would be restricted to £30,000 which is a good deal more acceptable than the £112,000 referred to above.

Further, more sophisticated planning arrangements can be made but they are exactly the same as apply to any other individual who is unmarried. It would of course be sensible to arrange on the first death for £154,000 of the deceased's estate to be transferred to a discretionary trust for the principal benefit of the survivor so that they are able to benefit from and enjoy the funds without it forming part of their estate for inheritance tax purposes. At £154,000, no tax arises and only the balance would pass to the survivor thereby limiting the tax payable on the second death.

Addresses

Relate, Herbert Gray College
Little Church Street, Rugby CV21 3AP. Tel: 01788 573241

Solicitors Family Law Association
P O Box 302, Keston, Kent BR2 6EZ. Tel: 01689 850227

Law Society
113 Chancery Lane, London WC2A 1JR. Tel: 0171 242 1222

Legal Services Ombudsman
22 Oxford Court, Manchester M2 3WQ.

Family and Divorce Centre
162 Tenison Road, Cambridge CB1 2DP. Tel: 01223 460136

National Family Mediation
The Chandley, 50 Westminster Bridge Road, London SE1 7Q7.
Tel: 0171 721 7658

Divorce Conciliation and Advisory Service
38 Ebury Street, London SW1W 0LU. Tel: 0171 730 2422

Index

accountants, 7, 8
accumulation and maintenance
    trust, 38–9
additional personal allowance,
    22–4
ancillary relief, 10, 46–52
Anton Piller order, 15–16, 51
Apsden v Hildsley 1981, 105
attachment of earnings order, 15

balance sheets, 125–6, 130–1
bankruptcy, 141–4
    insolvency, 140–2
beneficiaries, 36
Brooks v Brooks 1995, 119

Calderbank letter, 13–14, 65
capital gains tax, 30–1, 40, 164–7
    family companies, 137–9
charitable trust, 39
child care costs, 24–30
    crèches, 28
    nannies, 25–8
    self-employment, 29–30
Child Support Act 1991, 15, 57,
    77, 79, 81, 82, 83, 84
Child Support Agency, 11, 85
    bankruptcy, 142

family businesses, 144
    maintenance, 63, 66
Child Support Officers, 82, 83
children, 76–88
    excessive assessments avoidance,
        79–84
    with means, 84–7
    tax implications, 87–8
    see also child care; Child Support
Citizens Advice Bureaux, 6
clean break, 11, 56–7, 61
cohabitation, 152–69
    financial implications, 153–5
    inheritance and wills, 155–6
    maintenance entitlement, 157–8
    pre-nuptial and cohabitation
        agreements, 158–61
    taxation, 161–9; capital gains
        tax, 164–7; income tax,
        162–4; inheritance tax, 167–9
consent order, 10–11
crèches, 28
CSA *see* Child Support Agency

deferred charge, 103–4, 114–15
Department of Social Security, 77
discretionary trust, 38
Duxbury calculation, 14, 56, 60

family business, 122–40
  balance sheets, 125–6, 130–1
  family companies, 133–40
  goodwill, 125–6, 127–8
  lump sum, 130, 132
  price/earnings ratio, 128–9
  unincorporated businesses,
    124–33
family companies, 133–40
  capital gains tax, 137–9
family home, 89–116
  joint ownership, 96–9
  mortgage interest relief, 90–1
  order, types of, 99–104
  ownership problems, 91–6
  sale, 100
  tax implications, 104–16;
    deferred charge, 114–15;
    inheritance tax, 116; main
    residence exemption, 107–11;
    Mesher and Martin orders,
    113–14; sale or transfer to
    spouse, 111–13
Finance Act, 1988, 45
fixed interest trust, 37–8

goodwill, 125–6, 127–8

income tax, 19–21, 39, 162–4
inheritance, 155–6
Inheritance (Provision for Family
    and Dependants) Act 1975,
    11, 119, 149, 150, 156, 157
inheritance tax, 33–4, 41–2, 167–9
Inland Revenue
  attachment of earnings order, 15
  bankruptcy, 142
  children, 88
  cohabitation, 165

family home, 90, 103, 108, 109,
    111–12, 113, 114–15
  inheritance tax, 33
  maintenance, 46, 64
  pension rights, 119
  trusts, 39
  wills, 148
  see also taxation
Insolvency Act, 142
interim payments, 53
intestacy, 144–9
  no surviving spouse, 148–9
  survived by spouse but no issues,
    147
  survived by spouse and children,
    146–7

jargon, 9–16
  Anton Piller order, 15–16
  attachment of earnings order, 15
  Calderbank letter, 13–14
  clean break, 11
  consent order, 10–11
  Duxbury calculation, 14
  joint tenants: tenants in common,
    12
  McKenzie Friend, 16
  maintenance pending suit, 12
  Mareva injunction, 15–16
  Martin order, 15
  Mesher order, 14–15
  without prejudice, 12–13
joint tenants: tenants in common, 12
  judicial separation, 17–18

Law Reform Succession Bill, 157
legal advice, 6–7
lump sums, 57–60, 71–2
  Duxbury calculation, 60
  family business, 130, 132

McKenzie Friend, 16
main residence exemption, 107–11
maintenance, 43–75
  clean break, 56–7
  cohabitation, 157–8
  collection and enforcement, 63–5
  determination, 45–52; ancillary
    relief, 46–52
  foreign, 73–5
  and insolvency, 140–4
  lump sums, 57–60
  one-third rule, 54–6
  pending suit, 12, 52–3
  repeat applications, 61–2
  secured, 53
  taxation, 65–73; existing
    obligations, 66–7; lump sums,
    71–2; school fees, 72–3;
    secured maintenance, 67–71
  variation of orders, 60–2
Maintenance Enforcement Act,
  1991, 15
Mareva injunction, 15–16, 51
Marriage Guidance, 5–6
Married Women's Property Act
  1882, 93–4, 105, 112, 144,
  153, 154
Martin order, 15, 101, 113–14,
  115
Matrimonial Causes Act, 1973,
  46–7, 93, 117, 120
Matrimonial Property and
  Proceedings Act, 1970, 95
Mesher order, 14–15, 60, 100,
  101, 110, 113–14, 115
Mesher v Mesher, 1973, 14
mortgage interest relief, 90–1

nannies, 25–8
National Insurance contributions

  assessments, 81, 82
  child care costs, 27, 28
  maintenance, 55, 73

occupation rent, 103
one-third rule, 54–6
orders
  Anton Piller, 15–16, 51
  attachment of earnings, 15
  types of, 99–104
  variation of, 60–2
  see also Martin; Mesher
ownership problems, 91–6

pension rights, 117–21
personal allowance, 19–21
  additional, 22–4
pre-nuptial agreements, 158–61
price/earnings ratio, 128–9
problem areas identification, 1–3
professional advisers, 3–9

Relate, 5–6

school fees, 72–3
Scotland, 10, 149
self-employment, 29–30
separation agreements, 62
shareholders *see* family companies

taxation, 7–8, 19–42, 116
  additional personal allowance,
    22–4
  capital gains tax, 30–1
  child care costs, 24–30
  children, 87–8
  income tax, 19–21
  inheritance tax, 33–4
  traps of separation, avoidance of,
    31–3
  trusts, 34–7, 39–42; types, 37–9

see also cohabitation; family
home; Inland Revenue;
maintenance
Taxation of Chargeable Gains Act
1992, 110, 112
transfer to spouse, 102, 111–13
Trustee Act 1925, 85, 86
trustees, 36
trusts, 34–7
  beneficiaries, 36
  effect of, 36–7
  settlor, 35

trustees, 36
types, 37–9

unincorporated businesses,
124–33

Wachtel v. Wachtel 1973, 54
wills, 145–51, 155–6
  in existence, 149–51
  intestacy, 144–9
  mutual, 151
without prejudice, 12–13

All Pan Books are available at your local bookshop or newsagent, or can be ordered direct from the publisher. Indicate the number of copies required and fill in the form below.

Send to: Macmillan General Books C.S.
               Book Service By Post
               PO Box 29, Douglas I-O-M
               IM99 1BQ

or phone: 01624 675137, quoting title, author and credit card number.

or fax: 01624 670923, quoting title, author, and credit card number.

or Internet: http://www.bookpost.co.uk

Please enclose a remittance* to the value of the cover price plus 75 pence per book for post and packing. Overseas customers please allow £1.00 per copy for post and packing.

*Payment may be made in sterling by UK personal cheque, Eurocheque, postal order, sterling draft or international money order, made payable to Book Service By Post.

Alternatively by Access/Visa/MasterCard

Card No.

Expiry Date

Signature

Applicable only in the UK and BFPO addresses.

While every effort is made to keep prices low, it is sometimes necessary to increase prices at short notice. Pan Books reserve the right to show on covers and charge new retail prices which may differ from those advertised in the text or elsewhere.

NAME AND ADDRESS IN BLOCK CAPITAL LETTERS PLEASE

Name

Address

8/95

Please allow 28 days for delivery.
Please tick box if you do not wish to receive any additional information. ☐